Scoring for Films

UPDATED EDITION

A B O U T   T H I S   E D I T I O N:

Alfred has made every effort to make this book not only attractive but more useful and long-lasting as well. Usually, large books do not lie flat or stay open easily. In addition, the pages (which are glued together) tend to break away from the spine after repeated use.

In this edition, pages are sewn together in multiples of 16. This special process allows the book to stay open and prevents pages from falling out. We hope this unique binding will give you added pleasure and additional use.

D1496031

EARLE HAGEN

Alfred Publishing Co., Inc., Los Angeles

Alfred Publishing Co., Inc., 16380 Roscoe Blvd., Van Nuys, CA 91410-0003

ISBN: Softcover: 0-88284-387-7
Hardcover: 0-88284-388-5

3＝2

EXERCISE AND SELF-ANALYSIS FOR CHAPTER #1

Devise a large group of conversions from feet to seconds and vice-versa. Try to become so familiar with these simple conversions that you can do them automatically.

40 ft. = ? sec.

113 ft. = ? sec.

1 min. 23⅓ sec. – ?ft.

2 sec. = ? ft.

The formula is simple. Keep it that way. Always make sure that whatever answer you arrive at satisfies the ratio of 3 = 2.

3 (feet) = 2 (seconds).

2:15 1/3 sec = ?ft.

28 ft. = ?sec.

303 ft. = ?sec. (minutes and seconds)

With the advent of the pocket calculator, these simple examples become all too easy. However, the faster you become at calculating them, the quicker you will develop the necessary mechanics.

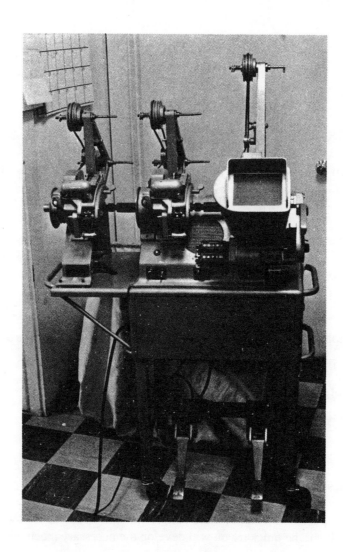

Example #2—A Three-Head Moviola

Example #2A—Ken Johnson, music editor, at work with the 3-Head Moviola

CHAPTER 2
THE PRIMARY EQUIPMENT

Before going further into the arithmetic, we should familiarize ourselves with the primary equipment we shall be using. Example #2 is a picture of a three-headed Moviola. The Moviola is a viewer apparatus that can show picture on the small ground glass viewer and run two or three aural tracks simultaneously. The aural tracks can be Mag Tracks—or Optically Recorded Tracks*. The mag and/or optical heads can be tied into a locked Synch (synchronization)*, or run separately. The functions of the Moviola are many and varied.

1st: It can be used as a viewer, with or without dialogue track. In the motion picture business, the picture and the dialogue are always recorded on separate pieces of equipment which are kept in step by a device called Synch Pulse*. The film only is run in the camera. A slate man stands in front of the camera with a small blackboard that has the film number and the individual take number written on it. On the signal to roll the camera, the slate man is photographed clapping a hinged board that is fastened to the top of the slate board. The slate man has announced the take number before clapping the boards. This gives the film editor a visual as well as aural alignment of his picture and dialogue tracks. After the picture has been developed, it is put into synch with the dialogue track by means of both the sight and sound of the slate man clapping the boards, and they are both coded by a machine which prints the footage on the edge of the picture and its mag track. In this way, the editor can keep his tracks in synch while cutting, and each track can be run separately by the picture, sound, and music editors.

2nd: On the Moviola, the composer can run the film fast or slow or a single frame at a time. This is the operation that the cutter goes through to give the composer his timings in 10ths or 3rds of seconds. Loops* or Click Tracks* can be checked as to picture or dialogue match.

3rd: The Moviola can be used after the recording to check the music tracks and make sure that they fit the picture.   *See glossary

THE MECHANICS AND VOCABULARY
OF
FILM COMPOSITION

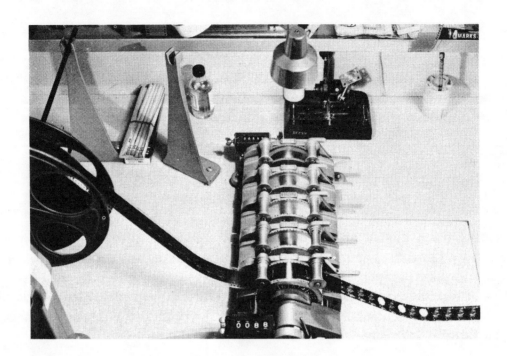

Example #3   Synch Machine

Example #3 is a picture of a synch machine. Synch, (synchronization) is one of the most used words in the film business. It applies to all branches of the editing crafts and indicates that the tracks involved are aligned synchronously from start to finish. The film editor, as he assembles his tracks, has to be sure that the dialogue tracks match the visual lip movements. The sound effects cutter must be sure that all of his sound effects match the visual. The Moviola is invaluable for sliding tracks back and forth until they are in synch. The tracks are then marked and placed in the synch machine. The synch machine is also used for building tracks for Dubbing*.

As you can see in Example #3, the synch machine is a device consisting of locked gears that revolve on a shaft. Above the gears are film clips that keep the gears engaged in the sprocket holes of the film. On the front gear shaft is a wheel that is marked in frames. This device is invaluable in the building of click tracks and will be discussed in detail later in the book.

*See glossary

Example #4—Dummy Machines

Example #4A—The recordist set-up.

THE MECHANICS AND VOCABULARY
OF
FILM COMPOSITION

Example #4B   Machine Room

Example #4B is a picture of the machine room in a film recording studio. The machines you see lined up are called Playback Dummies*. These machines do not record. They only play back. Their Playback* operations are electronically locked into synch with the stage projection machine. Any useable track is threaded up to a common Start Mark* in a dummy. As many dummies are used as the situation necessity calls for. It is possible to play back on the recording stage the picture, dialogue, sound, and as many music tracks as there are Pots* in the mixing panel. All of these tracks will be in synch with the picture. Dummies are also used to feed click tracks to the orchestra while recording. These tracks have a common start mark to the picture sequence and are piped to the conductor and the orchestra by means of Headsets*.

There are other pieces of equipment that will be used and we will discuss them as the need arises.

The mention of click tracks brings us to the subject of the next chapter.

*See glossary

CHAPTER 3
CLICK TRACKS

The most vital mechanical aid to the film composer is the click track. It is, in effect, a metronome. The primary advantage of the click track is that it is a synchronous metronome and is locked to the picture. Therefore, whatever beat speed is selected, the click track will perform in dead synch to the picture. This means that the composer can predetermine what cues he wants to catch, down to 1/384th of a second, and by means of the click track be assured that they will hit at the right place every time.

To understand what a click track is, let us examine more closely all of the kinds of mag track that are used in recording, discuss them in detail to understand their individual function, and then go through the procedure of building click tracks.

THE MECHANICS AND VOCABULARY
OF
FILM COMPOSITION

1

2

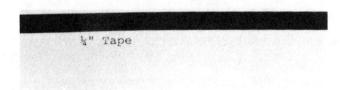

¼" Tape

3

Example #5
Mag Tracks

Example #5 shows the three kinds of mag track used in film recording.

#1 35MM full coat.

This mag track is used primarily for stereo recording and dubbing. Stereo film recording is called 3 STRIPE*, and has 3 separate bands recorded down the length of the film. At the moment, 3 stripe is not used much for film recording, especially in T.V. The T.V. broadcasting transmission is Monaural*. Consequently, the only time you would record on 3 stripe in T.V., is when you wish to simplify your orchestral balance problems. You would then have to Combine* your 3 stripe recording into a monaural track for further use. It is only a matter of time until T.V. goes to stereo recording. The transmission of F.M. stereo multiplexing broadcasting is excellent and it seems the next logical step for T.V. sound. At that time, 35 MM full coat for stereo will be used almost exclusively for recording. Record companies have gone to 35MM for better fidelity. Motion picture companies making pictures on 70MM record as much as six track stereo (Cinerama, Todd A-O).

#2 35MM Single Stripe.

This is used for almost all film recording that is to remain monaural. That, of course, takes in all of T.V. as it exists today.

#3 1/4″ Mag Tape.

This track is used for Wild* takes and for protection. 1/4 inch track cannot be played back with the picture because it has no sprocket holes and therefore cannot be locked into synch with the picture. 1/4 inch is used primarily for wild recording when there are no picture facilities. It is also used as a general protection tape when the other kinds of mag track are being used. Occasionally there will be Drop-outs*, rips, stretching, or high noise level on the 35MM mag. Because most 1/4 inch machines in the film recording studios have Synch Pulse*, you simply transfer the take to a new 35MM mag. This can be done at the end of the recording session and save you time on the stage. Drop-outs occur when you record across a piece of 35MM mag that is perhaps unevenly coated. The sudden drop in level makes the recorded track unuseable. T.V. companies do not always use new mag tape. Some of them prefer to save the expense of about $30.00 a roll and de-magnetize the 35MM and use it over again. Sometimes there are splices in the reclaimed tape that will pop when you play them back. Once again, all you have to do is play the 1/4 inch and if the take is O.K., order a reprint and go on. You might wonder why it wouldn't be easier to record another take. If you consider the fact that you might have a tape failure in an excellently recorded tape of a difficult piece of music, you can see that the 1/4 inch protects the performance as well as saving time. In addition, the 1/4 inch is usually stored. If the track is damaged or torn the cutter can give the recording company the picture identification and number of the take, then a transfer to 35 mag can be made in a matter of minutes.

See glossary

THE MECHANICS AND VOCABULARY
OF
FILM COMPOSITION

If you examine the properties of the film base you are going to be working with, Example #1, you will find that the optical film and the 35MM mag tracks, (full coat and single stripe) have only one thing in common — the sprocket holes down the sides. These perforations in the optical and mag tracks are identical and serve the same purpose. The sprockets that are driven by the projectors, dummies, advance the film and tracks by turning into these perforations — much the same as a bicycle sprocket engages the chain. As long as the projector is running, all other tracks that are in lock with the projector will be driven at the same speed.

While the mag tracks have no frames, you will notice that optical film has four sprocket holes to each frame of picture. Actually, the division of the frame starts between holes as shown in Example #1. Therefore, we also refer to the distance of four sprocket holes, on mag tracks, as 1 frame.

Take a piece of opaque leader and put it into a synch machine along with the picture. Mark a line with a white marking pen on the leader corresponding to the first frame of picture. You now have a synchronous start mark for picture and track. With a hand punch, punch a hole on the line of the leader. Run the leader through the synch machine for 24 frames and punch it again. As you roll the leader through the synch machine, the picture will travel with it. Punch a hole every 24 frames until the picture sequence ends. You have now built yourself a 24 frame click track to match the picture. As the punch mark runs over the optical playback head, it will make an audible pop. This pop is played to the conductor and the orchestra by means of a one piece headset (earphone). These headsets are run off of a line from the control booth. The constant pop of 24 frames a second would act as a metronome for the orchestra and they would be playing to a metronome value of M.M. = 60 (metronome marking) at 1 beat per second.

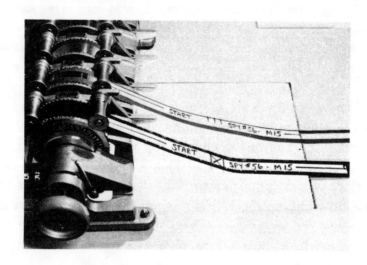

Example #6   The Start Mark

To prepare this click track for the stage, the cutter puts a 20-foot piece of blank leader on both the picture and click track and marks both with a tape with the proper sequence number written on it. For instance, M11. Music-Reel 1, Part 1. The first digit refers to the number of the reel, the second to the sequence in that reel. M34 would be Music-Reel 3, Part 4. On the recording stage, the recordist marks his mag track with a piece of tape and writes the corresponding take number on it. The stage monitor man speaks into a microphone and "slates" the take. "I SPY", Show #56, M 15, Take 1". This completely identifies the show, the sequence, and the take. The house lights dim, the projectionist starts the projector and the dummy machine and the 35MM mag recorder roll in perfect synch. When the take is over, the projectionist and the recordist rewind their machines to the original start mark and the dummy operator disengages his lock to get off of the playback line. Again at a signal from the stage monitor, the projectionist starts his machine and the recorder, which has been set to "playback", rolls with him. But this time you hear the recorded track played back over the studio speakers.

To start the orchestra playing when they hear the click track in their headsets, the cutter will put on a predesignated amount of clicks from the first frame of picture backwards into the 20 foot leader. If the music is in 4/4 or 2/4, he will generally use 8 Warning Clicks*. If the music is in 3s or 5s, he will use 9 or 10 warning clicks. If the click is very fast he will usually double the amount of the warning clicks. This gives the orchestra a chance to get prepared. The composer usually indicates on the score what he wants and informs the orchestra as to how many warning clicks they have. He may even count them out loud.

This procedure has been very detailed in case you do not have a music cutter working with you. By following this procedure you can take care of all the necessary preparation. You can also build click tracks without a synch machine. You punch a hole on the line of the first frame of picture, then count 4 sprocket holes for as many frames as you need to punch the next.

There is a second kind of click track that you can use.

This click track is called a Loop*. To make a loop, the cutter punches out even clicks for about 6 feet. He then splices the two ends together to form a loop. This loop runs continuously in the dummy providing the orchestra with a never ending click. The conductor counts a couple of bars and the orchestra plays. Because there is no start mark for a loop, it is used exclusively for wild recording. This method of clicks is used extensively. There are budget-conscious operations that will not spend the money for picture recording. These operations use loops and stop watch almost entirely. On the modern recording stage, the loop has been replaced by the Digital Click Machine*. This machine can provide clicks in 1/2 hole units for any given beat from 1/2 hole to 99-7 frames.

The loop, however, remains a vital part of the mechanics of breaking down a picture and almost any music cutter has a complete set of loops in stock at all times.

We will cover this as we get deeper into clk. (click) tks. (tracks).

See glossary

Example 7A is a view of the engineer's booth and shows the recording console with its complex of controls.

Attempting to explain all of the functions of this recording console would require a book in itself. No two recording studios use identical set-ups, so familiarize yourself with the capabilities of the one with which you will be working.

Example #7A
John Norman, engineer, at the control panel
Stage M, Glen Glenn Sound Services, Paramount Studios, Hollywood, Calif.

Example 7B is a typical motion picture recording set up. The photograph shows the conductor's stand facing the screen. The podium has a large stop clock, a microphone to the booth to instruct the recording engineer, a head set with volume controls that enables the conductor to hear clicks, dialogue, vocal tracks, or the orchestra mix as it will be recorded.

Example #7B   Recording Stage:
Conductor's Stand, Music Editor's and Slate Man's Table.

(Stage M)

To the right of the conductor's stand is the music editor's and slate man's table. The left side of this table is occupied by the music editor and contains the digital click track machine and a remote control start, stop, and re-set control for the stop clock. Ex. 7D is a close up of the digital machine.

The middle panel of this table is the engineer's playback panel and can play four or more tracks in synch with the picture. This panel is used only for playing back takes as the engineer is in a soundproof booth during the actual take.

The panel on the right is the control for the slate man to audibly number the takes and to notify the system, via intercom, that the conductor is ready to start recording.

Example #7C   The Music Editor's Table

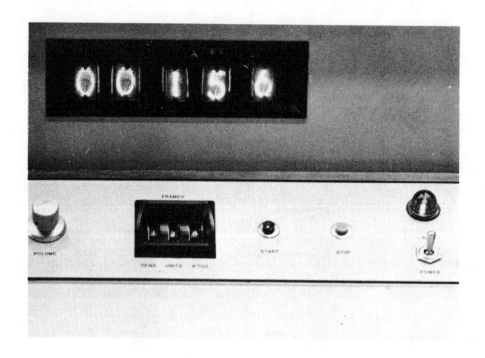

Example #7D   The Digital Click Loop Machine

Example #7E

One of the newest and most modern film recording stages in the world.
Stage M, Glen Glenn Sound Services, Paramount Studios, Hollywood, Calif.

THE MECHANICS AND VOCABULARY
OF
FILM COMPOSITION

Example #7F

The recording booth—from the stage viewpoint

Example #7G

Motion Picture Orchestra Recording Set-up

Example #7H

The Main Recording Console (Stage M)

Example #7I

Patch Bay (Stage M)

Example #7J

Part of the dummy playback system (Stage M)

Example #7K

Fully automated forwards and backwards running projector (Stage M)

VIDEO (SMPTE time code)

In a good many of today's studios, especially the smaller ones used for video, you will see television monitors rather than screens for projection. These studios deal mostly in video equipment using SMPTE time code. SMPTE (Society of Motion Picture and Television Engineers) time code is a method of supplying video tape with electronic sprocket holes. Inasmuch as this book is about film and not video tape, I will leave the explanation of the workings of video to others in that field. Video is being used more and more in the editing of film. There is equipment that will allow you to use film mechanics in adapting music to video. The synthesizer field uses SMPTE time code almost exclusively. In my estimation, working with film gives you, the composer, the most flexibility for creative and dramatic opportunity at this point in time.

THE MECHANICS AND VOCABULARY
OF
FILM COMPOSITION

CHAPTER 4
THE MECHANICS OF CLICK TRACKS

Referring back to our previous chapter, we know that our 24 frame click track will give us a beat a second—Metronome 60. It is logical that if we make our punch mark every 12 frames instead of 24, we will double the tempo. Each click will be 1/2 second apart, M.M.=120. You can bet that if you have a marching band sequence to score, the tempo will be pretty close to a 12 frame click. M.M.=120 is the standard metronome time for march tempo. College bands march somewhat faster; military bands slightly slower. Your picture needs, however, can be matched <u>exactly</u>.

Where the picture editor must work in single frame units, because he can not cut into the middle of a visual frame, the composer and the music cutter can and do deal in fractional units as small as 1/2 of a sprocket hole. Example #8 shows a frame of optical track film and the details of how music can break this frame into fractional units. Obviously, the closer together the punches, the faster the tempo. Our units need not be in whole frames only, so we develop a new film language that is peculiar to music cutting. The dividing line is the start of the frame. The first hole is unit 1. The space between the first and second hole is unit 2. The second hole is unit 3. And so on until we get to the last hole. This is unit 7. The next space between holes is the start of the next frame. If we refer to a march sequence as a 12-2 click, the cutter will punch out 12 frames and two 1/2 holes.

**Optical
Sound
Track**

Frame Line (between holes)

1 hole . . . . unit #1

1/2 hole . . . . unit #2

hole . . . . unit #3

1/2 hole . . . . unit #4

hole . . . . unit #5

1/2 hole . . . . unit #6

hole . . . . unit #7

Frame Line

EXAMPLE #8

Subdivision of a Frame of Film for a Fractional Click Track.

THE MECHANICS AND VOCABULARY
OF
FILM COMPOSITION

There are many reasons for using these unit divisions of a frame and the best way to investigate them is to start with a specific picture obligation.

Assume we have a sequence where there are people visually dancing. The problem is to put music to the sequence in exactly the tempo that the people are dancing.

When the film is shot, the production company will play a Guide Track* on the stage to start the people dancing. Just before the dialogue starts, an operator will shut off the "guide" track so that the music will not be recorded on the dialogue track. As long as the dialogue track is recorded Clean*, (by itself) the dialogue track and picture can be edited without having to worry about cutting parts of musical beats, or having jumps in music. It becomes the composers problem to put the music back into the picture so that it has continuity from start to finish and at the same time matches the tempo of the people who are dancing. The guide track might be a commercial record, a Pre-recorded Track*, or simply a click record to provide a tempo. In some cases the orchestra might be visible in the scene. This adds to the composers problems. Beside having to match tempo, he must also write music that will match what the orchestra seems to be playing. The orchestra will look visually as though they are playing (Sideline)*, but in fact they will not be making a sound. Any audible sound would be picked up on the dialogue track and create big editing problems. What do we do? — Head for the Moviola.

First of all, with a stop watch, you can rough time four bars of the visual tempo.

Look up the four bar tempo on the click track chart, Example #9, and pick the nearest click to the chart reference. It was mentioned before that the cutter usually keeps a complete set of loops in stock. These loops are smaller than the ones that are used in the recording dummies as they only have to be large enough to go around the head of a Moviola. These loops are usually boxed according to frames. For example, a box of 11 frame loops will contain all the loops from 11 frames to an 11-7 in 1/2 hole units.

Let us suppose that the rough tempo of the dancing looked to be about 4 bars of 4/4 in 7 seconds. This was the stop watch timing. This is a good time to advise you that a good pocket stop watch, in 1/5th of seconds, is an absolute must for the film composer. In any event, we look at the click track chart for the click corresponding to 4 bars of 4/4 in 7 seconds, and find that it is a 10-4 click. We select a 10-4 loop and thread it in the Moviola so that a punch falls on the first frame of the picture sequence. If the first few bars of the guide track were recorded before the track was turned off for dialogue, we can use that as a further reference for tempo. With the loop in place, we start the Moviola at regular speed. We see the picture and hear the beats of the click. Assume that the click and the picture seem to be together for a few bars and then the click seems to pull ahead. This indicates that we have too fast a loop so we rewind the picture to the start and try a slower loop. This time let's try a 10-6 click, and assume that this time the tempo seems to hold a bit longer and then starts to fall behind. We have now bracketed the tempo so we try the 10-5, the one in between.

*See glossary

EXAMPLE #9

CLICK TRACK CHART

FRAMES	4 BARS of 2/4	4 BARS of 3/4	4 BARS of 4/4	32 BARS of 2/4	32 BARS of 3/4	32 BARS of 4/4	METRONOME
6	2	3	4	16	24	32	
6-1	2.04	3.06	4.08	16.33	24.5	32.66	
6-2	2.08	3.12	4.17	16.66	25	33.33	
6-3	2.12	3.18	4.25	17	25.5	34	
6-4	2.16	3.24	4.33	17.33	26	34.66	
6-5	2.2	3.30	4.42	17.66	26.5	35.33	
6-6	2.25	3.37	4.5	18	27	36	
6-7	2.29	3.43	4.58	18.33	27.5	36.66	208
7	2.33	3.5	4.67	18.66	28	37.33	
7-1	2.37	3.56	4.75	19	28.5	38	200
7-2	2.41	3.62	4.83	19.33	29	38.66	
7-3	2.45	3.68	4.92	19.66	29.5	39.33	
7-4	2.5	3.75	5	20	30	40	192
7-5	2.54	3.81	5.08	20.33	30.5	40.66	
7-6	2.58	3.87	5.17	20.66	31	41.33	
7-7	2.62	3.93	5.25	21	31.5	42	184
8	2.66	3.99	5.33	21.33	32	42.66	
8-1	2.71	4.05	5.42	21.66	32.5	43.33	
8-2	2.75	4.12	5.5	22	33	44	176
8-3	2.79	4.18	5.58	22.33	33.5	44.66	
8-4	2.83	4.24	5.67	22.66	34	45.33	168
8-5	2.87	4.30	5.75	23	34.5	46	
8-6	2.91	4.36	5.83	23.33	35	46.66	
8-7	2.96	4.40	5.92	23.66	35.5	47.33	
9	3	4.5	6	24	36	48	160
9-1	3.04	4.56	6.08	24.33	36.5	48.66	
9-2	3.08	4.62	6.17	24.66	37	49.33	
9-3	3.12	4.68	6.25	25	37.5	50	
9-4	3.16	4.74	6.33	25.33	38	50.66	152
9-5	3.2	4.8	6.42	25.66	38.5	51.33	
9-6	3.25	4.87	6.5	26	39	52	
9-7	3.29	4.93	6.58	26.33	39.5	52.66	
10	3.33	4.99	6.67	26.66	40	53.33	144
10-1	3.37	5.05	6.75	27	40.5	54	
10-2	3.41	5.12	6.83	27.33	41	54.66	
10-3	3.45	5.18	6.92	27.66	41.5	55.33	
10-4	3.5	5.25	7	28	42	56	138
10-5	3.54	5.31	7.08	28.33	42.5	56.66	
10-6	3.58	5.37	7.17	28.66	43	57.33	132
10-7	3.62	5.43	7.25	29	43.5	58	
11	3.66	5.49	7.33	29.33	44	58.66	
11-1	3.71	5.55	7.42	29.66	44.5	59.33	
11-2	3.75	5.62	7.5	30	45	60	
11-3	3.79	5.68	7.58	30.33	45.5	60.66	
11-4	3.83	5.74	7.67	30.66	46	61.33	126
11-5	3.87	5.80	7.75	31	46.5	62	
11-6	3.91	5.86	7.83	31.33	47	62.66	
11-7	3.96	5.92	7.92	31.66	47.5	63.33	
12	4	6	8	32	48	64	120
12-1	4.04	6.06	8.08	32.33	48.5	64.66	
12-2	4.08	6.12	8.17	32.66	49	65.33	
12-3	4.12	6.18	8.25	33	49.5	66	116
12-4	4.16	6.24	8.33	33.33	50	66.66	
12-5	4.2	6.30	8.42	33.66	50.5	67.33	
12-6	4.25	6.37	8.5	34	51	68	112
12-7	4.29	6.43	8.58	34.33	51.5	68.66	
13	4.33	6.5	8.67	34.66	52	69.33	
13-1	4.37	6.56	8.75	35	52.5	70	
13-2	4.41	6.62	8.83	35.33	53	70.66	108
13-3	4.45	6.68	8.92	35.66	53.5	71.33	
13-4	4.5	6.75	9	36	54	72	
13-5	4.54	6.81	9.08	36.33	54.5	72.66	
13-6	4.58	6.87	9.17	36.66	55	73.33	104

EXAMPLE #9 (Cont.)
CLICK TRACK CHART

FRAMES	4 BARS of 2/4	4 BARS of 3/4	4 BARS of 4/4	32 BARS of 2/4	32 BARS of 3/4	32 BARS of 4/4	METRONOME
13-7	4.62	6.93	9.25	37	55.5	74	
14	4.66	6.99	9.33	37.33	56	74.66	
14-1	4.71	7.05	9.42	37.66	56.5	75.33	
14-2	4.75	7.12	9.5	38	57	76	100
14-3	4.79	7.18	9.58	38.33	57.5	76.66	
14-4	4.83	7.24	9.67	38.66	58	77.33	
14-5	4.87	7.30	9.75	39	58.5	78	
14-6	4.91	7.36	9.83	39.33	59	78.66	
14-7	4.96	7.40	9.92	39.66	59.5	79.33	
15	5	7.5	10	40	60	80	96
15-1	5.04	7.56	10.08	40.33	60.5	80.66	
15-2	5.08	7.62	10.17	40.66	61	81.33	
15-3	5.12	7.68	10.25	41	61.5	82	
15-4	5.16	7.74	10.33	41.33	62	82.66	
15-5	5.2	7.8	10.42	41.66	62.5	83.33	
15-6	5.25	7.87	10.5	42	63	84	92
15-7	5.29	7.93	10.58	42.33	63.5	84.66	
16	5.33	7.99	10.67	42.66	64	85.33	
16-1	5.37	8.05	10.75	43	64.5	86	
16-2	5.41	8.12	10.83	43.33	65	86.66	88
16-3	5.45	8.18	10.92	43.66	65.5	87.33	
16-4	5.5	8.25	11	44	66	88	
16-5	5.54	8.31	11.08	44.33	66.5	88.66	
16-6	5.58	8.37	11.17	44.66	67	89.33	
16-7	5.62	8.43	11.25	45	67.5	90	
17	5.66	8.49	11.33	45.33	68	90.66	
17-1	5.71	8.55	11.42	45.66	68.5	91.33	
17-2	5.75	8.62	11.5	46	69	92	84
17-3	5.79	8.68	11.58	46.33	69.5	92.66	
17-4	5.83	8.74	11.67	46.66	70	93.33	
17-5	5.87	8.80	11.75	47	70.5	94	
17-6	5.91	8.86	11.83	47.33	71	94.66	
17-7	5.96	8.92	11.92	47.66	71.5	95.33	
18	6	9	12	48	72	96	80
18-1	6.04	9.06	12.08	48.33	72.5	96.66	
18-2	6.08	9.12	12.17	48.66	73	97.33	
18-3	6.12	9.18	12.25	49	73.5	98	
18-4	6.16	9.24	12.33	49.33	74	98.66	
18-5	6.2	9.30	12.42	49.66	74.5	99.33	
18-6	6.25	9.37	12.5	50	75	100	76
18-7	6.29	9.43	12.58	50.33	75.5	100.66	
19	6.33	9.5	12.67	50.66	76	101.33	
19-1	6.37	9.56	12.75	51	76.5	102	
19-2	6.41	9.62	12.83	51.33	77	102.66	
19-3	6.45	9.68	12.92	51.66	77.5	103.33	
19-4	6.5	9.75	13	52	78	104	
19-5	6.54	9.81	13.08	52.33	78.5	104.66	
19-6	6.58	9.87	13.17	52.66	79	105.33	
19-7	6.62	9.93	13.25	53	79.5	106	
20	6.66	9.99	13.33	53.33	80	106.66	72
20-1	6.71	10.05	13.42	53.66	80.5	107.33	
20-2	6.75	10.12	13.5	54	81	108	
20-3	6.79	10.18	13.58	54.33	81.5	108.66	
20-4	6.83	10.24	13.67	54.66	82	109.33	
20-5	6.87	10.30	13.75	55	82.5	110	
20-6	6.91	10.36	13.83	55.33	83	110.66	69
20-7	6.96	10.4	13.92	55.66	83.5	111.33	
21	7	10.5	14	56	84	112	
21-1	7.04	10.56	14.08	56.33	84.5	112.66	
21-2	7.08	10.62	14.17	56.66	85	113.33	
21-3	7.12	10.68	14.25	57	85.5	114	
21-4	7.16	10.74	14.33	57.33	86	114.66	
21-5	7.2	10.8	14.42	57.66	86.5	115.33	
21-6	7.25	10.87	14.5	58	87	116	66
21-7	7.29	10.93	14.58	58.33	87.5	116.66	
22	7.33	10.99	14.67	58.66	88	117.33	
22-1	7.37	11.05	14.75	59	88.5	118	
22-2	7.41	11.12	14.83	59.33	89	118.66	
22-3	7.45	11.18	14.92	59.66	89.5	119.33	
22-4	7.5	11.25	15	60	90	120	
22-5	7.54	11.31	15.08	60.33	90.5	120.66	
22-6	7.58	11.37	15.17	60.33	90.5	120.66	

EXAMPLE #9 (Cont.)
CLICK TRACK CHART

FRAMES	4 BARS of 2/4	4 BARS of 3/4	4 BARS of 4/4	32 BARS of 2/4	32 BARS of 3/4	32 BARS of 4/4	METRONOME
20	6.66	9.99	13.33	53.33	80	106.66	72
20-1	6.71	10.05	13.42	53.66	80.5	107.33	
20-2	6.75	10.12	13.5	54	81	108	
20-3	6.79	10.18	13.58	54.33	81.5	108.66	
20-4	6.83	10.24	13.67	54.66	82	109.33	
20-5	6.87	10.30	13.75	55	82.5	110	
20-6	6.91	10.36	13.83	55.33	83	110.66	69
20-7	6.96	10.4	13.92	55.66	83.5	111.33	
21	7	10.5	14	56	84	112	
21-1	7.04	10.56	14.08	56.33	84.5	112.66	
21-2	7.08	10.62	14.17	56.66	85	113.33	
21-3	7.12	10.68	14.25	57	85.5	114	
21-4	7.16	10.74	14.33	57.33	86	114.66	
21-5	7.2	10.8	14.42	57.66	86.5	115.33	
21-6	7.25	10.87	14.5	58	87	116	66
21-7	7.29	10.93	14.58	58.33	87.5	116.66	
22	7.33	10.99	14.67	58.66	88	117.33	
22-1	7.37	11.05	14.75	59	88.5	118	
22-2	7.41	11.12	14.83	59.33	89	118.66	
22-3	7.45	11.18	14.92	59.66	89.5	119.33	
22-4	7.5	11.25	15	60	90	120	
22-5	7.54	11.31	15.08	60.33	90.5	120.66	
22-6	7.58	11.37	15.17	60.66	91	121.33	63
22-7	7.62	11.43	15.25	61	91.5	122	
23	7.66	11.49	15.33	61.33	92	122.66	
23-1	7.71	11.55	15.42	61.66	92.5	123.33	
23-2	7.75	11.62	15.5	62	93	124	
23-3	7.79	11.68	15.58	62.33	93.5	124.66	
23-4	7.83	11.74	15.67	62.66	94	125.33	
23-5	7.87	11.80	15.75	63	94.5	126	
23-6	7.91	11.86	15.83	63.33	95	126.66	
23-7	7.96	11.92	15.92	63.66	95.5	127.33	
24	8	12	16	64	96	128	60
24-1	8.04	12.06	16.08	64.33	96.5	128.66	
24-2	8.08	12.12	16.17	64.66	97	129.33	
24-3	8.12	12.18	16.25	65	97.5	130	
24-4	8.16	12.24	16.33	65.33	98	130.66	
24-5	8.2	12.30	16.42	65.66	98.5	131.33	
24-6	8.25	12.37	16.5	66	99	132	58
24-7	8.29	12.43	16.58	66.33	99.5	132.66	
25	8.33	12.5	16.67	66.66	100	133.33	
25-1	8.37	12.56	16.75	67	100.5	134	
25-2	8.41	12.62	16.83	67.33	101	134.66	
25-3	8.45	12.68	16.92	67.66	101.5	135.33	
25-4	8.5	12.75	17	68	102	136	
25-5	8.54	12.81	17.08	68.33	102.5	136.66	
25-6	8.58	12.87	17.17	68.66	103	137.33	56
25-7	8.62	12.93	17.25	69	103.5	138	
26	8.66	12.99	17.33	69.33	104	138.66	
26-1	8.71	13.05	17.42	69.66	104.5	139.33	
26-2	8.75	13.12	17.5	70	105	140	
26-3	8.79	13.18	17.58	70.33	105.5	140.66	
26-4	8.83	13.24	17.67	70.66	106	141.33	
26-5	8.87	13.30	17.75	71	106.5	142	
26-6	8.91	13.36	17.83	71.33	107	142.66	54
26-7	8.96	13.40	17.92	71.66	107.5	143.33	
27	9	13.5	18	72	108	144	
27-1	9.04	13.56	18.08	72.33	108.5	144.66	
27-2	9.08	13.62	18.17	72.66	109	145.33	
27-3	9.12	13.68	18.25	73	109.5	146	
27-4	9.16	13.74	18.33	73.33	110	146.66	
27-5	9.2	13.80	18.42	73.66	110.5	147.33	
27-6	9.25	13.87	18.5	74	111	148	52
27-7	9.29	13.93	18.58	74.33	111.5	148.66	
28	9.33	13.99	18.67	74.66	112	149.33	

More than likely, this is the correct click and will hold through the sequence. Although the difference between the two is infinitesimal, 1/192th of a second per beat, the longer the piece goes on, the more discrepancy will accumulate. For example, 150 beats of a 10-6 loop is 1 minute, 6.74 seconds (1:06.74). 150 beats of a 10-5 loop is 1:05.97. There is almost 2/3rds of a second variation over 150 beats. As we know from our 3=2 formula, 2/3rds of a second is 16 frames. That is, in this example, we are more than one full beat out of synch, and 2 frames out of synch is noticeably annoying and visually wrong. This gives you some idea of how exact this business has to be. If suddenly in this sequence the tempo seems to jump to an afterbeat, or part of a beat, and holds tempo, you can be sure that the film editor has cut the picture out of tempo. Examine the film closely at a reduced speed and find the cut where the picture goes off. Talk to the film editor and have him trim the film properly. The most that he would have to add or trim would be 1/2 of a single beat. In this case, 5 frames. This is easy to do and most film editors are extremely cooperative.

This is a simple and common problem that you run into all of the time. Others of course will come to mind: marching bands, singing, dancing, walking sequences, etc. All of these offer problems that can be solved by this procedure.

There is one final problem to consider when you are matching clicks to a visual sequence. Beside finding the matching clicks, you must also determine the bar line. This is to say that you must not only find the right beat that the people are dancing to, but the downbeats of the bars as well. If you have any of the guide track to refer to, your problem is simplified. If not, this is still not much of a problem. You can tell pretty well by the movements of the people where the down beat of the bar is. In a marching band sequence, you want to get the 1st and 3rd beats on the left foot. When you lay out the click track, you may find that you have part of an incomplete bar in front to get the downbeat to fall properly. Any part of an incomplete bar in front is usually labeled an "A" bar. The cutter lines up his clicks to the "A" bar and labels the exact start of the cue as :00. This is hard to explain with words, but easy with an example.

The procedure from the time you determine the tempo is as follows:

Example #10 is a Bar Breakdown* that contains an "A" bar, orchestra action, and the general description of what is taking place.

Example #11 is the bar breakdown executed.

As you can see, the vital information is at the top of the page. The picture number (in this case a television sequence), the title (for copyright purpose), the cue number, the click, and the warning clicks involved. Starting with the "A" bar, all of the clicks are numbered, and all of the action, including dialogue, is carefully and completely detailed. The composer can write or sketch directly on the breakdown and know that what he writes will fit the picture exactly. It is very important that you keep a metronome, preferably electric, handy at all times when working with clicks. Check the click tempo often when you write. The end result must sound perfectly natural. Checking the tempo with a metronome is good insurance.

See glossary

■ .9.4 CLIX METRO = 152 Title   **EXAMPLE #10**

RUNNING BEATS

4 BARS $\frac{4}{4}$ = .06$\frac{1}{3}$ 8 FREE TO D.B. - ■■ ("I SPY" #13, M-34)

■■ BARS TO GET STARTED
2.

Composer

Arranger   ①

← EXTRA BARS TO GET STARTED ——→

Ⓒ   Ⓑ

■ 1:00
CENTER OF DISS.
TO NITE EXT.
MAMA SAN's PLACE

ACTUAL START
OF
CUE

Ⓐ   ①   ■   ①

Prod. _____   Title   EXAMPLE #10 (Cont.)   Composer _____   ②
                                                          Arranger _____

.06

K + S ENTER SCENE
↓
+ WALK TO
ENTRANCE
15   19   23   27

④   ⑤   ⑥   ⑦

.12⅓

THEY ENTER
↓

CUT TO INT.
GEISHA GIRLS
→ DANCERS

31   35   39   43

⑧   ⑨   ⑩   ⑪

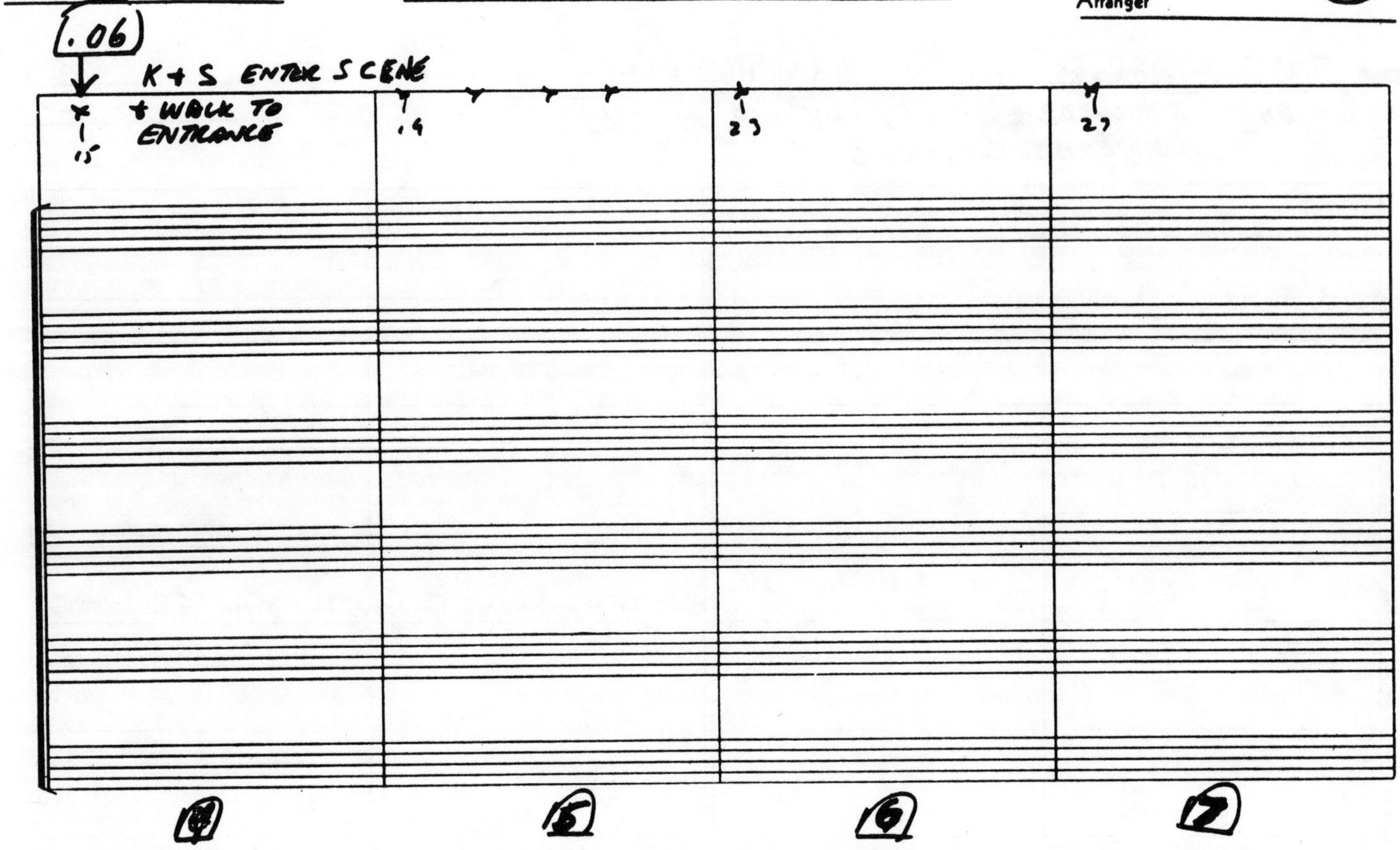

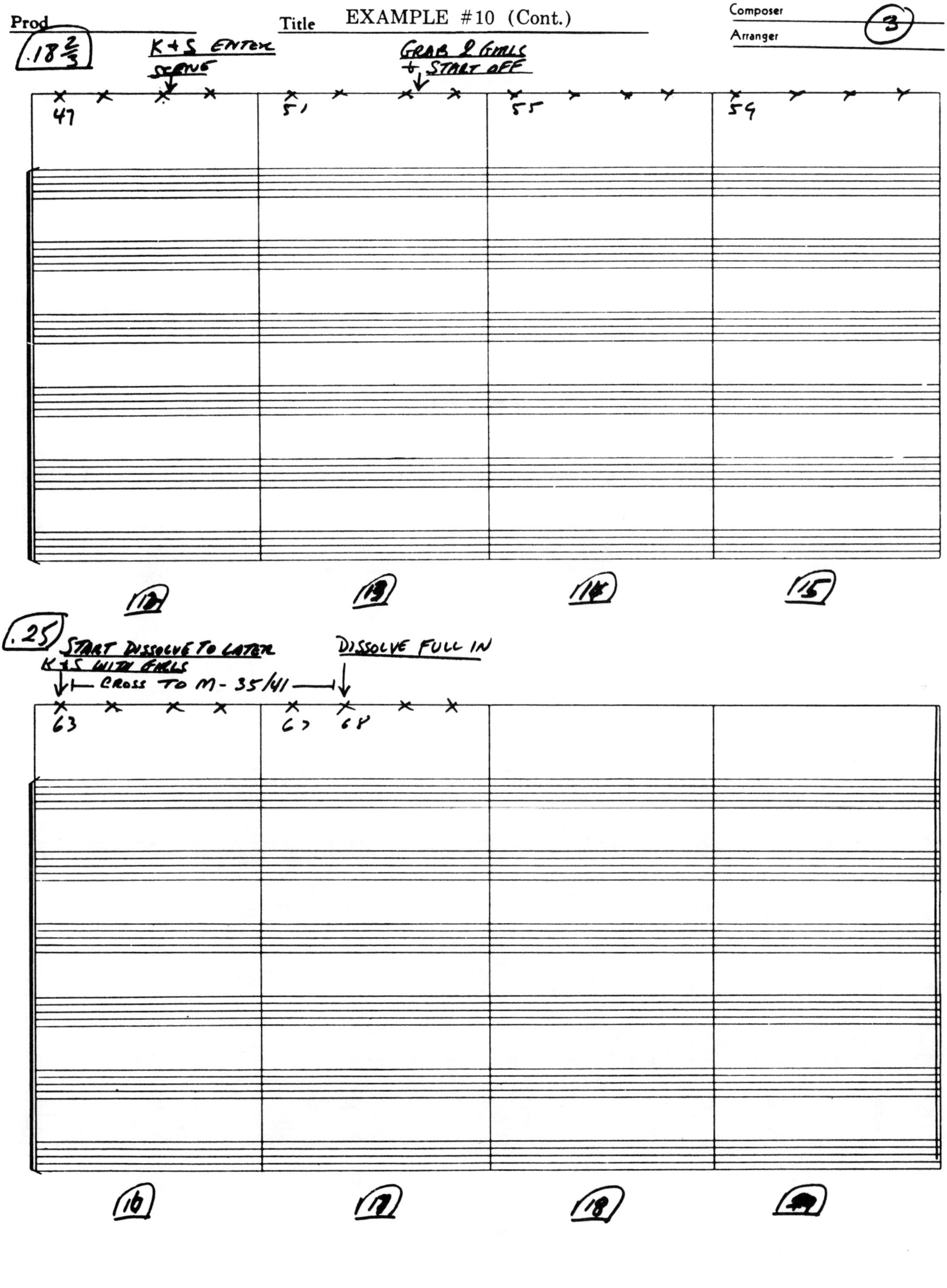

Prod

.18 2/3

Title   EXAMPLE #10 (Cont.)

Composer

Arranger   3

K+S ENTER
SCENE

GRAB 2 GIRLS
+ START OFF

47   51   55   59

12   13   14   15

.25   START DISSOLVE TO LATER
K+S WITH GIRLS
CROSS TO M - 35/41

DISSOLVE FULL IN

63   67   68

16   17   18   20

Prod. _____ Title __EXAMPLE #11 (Cont.)__ Composer ___ ③
Arranger ___

Clicks may be used to satisfy the composer's desires even though the picture does not demand a click obligation. For example, in a comedy scene, you might want to score a sequence where you want the music to catch direct pieces of action. In this instance you can remove the human frailities of conducting, playing, and holding strict tempos in the orchestra, by use of the click track. In some cases, there will be action tempo that you can use to musical advantage. You can have the cutter give you a click track breakdown in the tempo of the action. An aerialist swinging back and forth on a trapeze has a tempo. It can be matched, and you may want to write on it. A child bouncing a ball, a train, people running, etc. — anything that has tempo — can be caught.

Animation involves the highest usage of click tracks. Practically all cartoon music is done to click tracks. In many instances the music is recorded first and animated later. When it comes to what we call "Mickey Mouse" music, where everything in sight is caught, the best examples are in the medium that developed clicks — cartoons — hence, "Mickey Mouse".

*   *   *

So far this book has dealt with ideal conditions. In order to control your medium you have to assume that there will be more times when the conditions are anything but ideal. Perhaps you will be assigned a music cutter who has little experience in bar breakdowns; perhaps you will be working independently with no cutter available; perhaps you will be working at home with a cue sheet and decide to use a click. All of these situations are real. They happen all of the time. The answer as to what to do and how to do it comes from further knowledge of the mechanics.

If you should decide to use a click track while you are working at home, don't forget to relay the information to your music editor. The specifics of the click track have to be given to the music editor so that he can build the cue for the recording. The information must then be passed on to those people who will be working with it on the recording stage. If you are working without a music editor, then it is up to you to get the information to the recording stage. The next chapter, which deals with the "Bible," should help make this clear.

THE MECHANICS AND VOCABULARY
OF
FILM COMPOSITION

CHAPTER 5

THE BREAKDOWN OF A FILM

In order to proceed, we must discuss the physical breakdown of a film. We won't cover the psychological aspects as yet.

We will assume that you have run your film in a projection room or on the Moviola. You have decided where you are going to Spot* your music. You have told the cutter where you want the music cues to start and stop. The cutter starts preparing a cue-by-cue breakdown. Each cue is given a sequential number according to its place in the reel and the picture. M 11 is Music-Reel 1, Part 1. M 12 is Music-Reel 1, Part 2, and so on. The cutter, or you, then proceed to time out the cues in detail. If there are bar breakdowns needed, he prepares them. If he is not able, you have to do it. All other cues will be prepared and typewritten. The cues are timed to the nearest 1/3rd of a second. We use 1/3rds because they are the smallest fraction of a second that a conductor can catch with a stopwatch and because 1/3rd of a second is generally close enough to match the picture. In the case of a cue that is extremely critical, you might want your timings in 10th's. 10th's of a second usually necessitates clicks as it is not possible to accurately catch a 10th with the baton. In any event, a day or two after breakdown you would begin to get your complete set of cues assembled. When you have them all, you should also get a master list showing all of the cues and the timing of each. Example #12 shows a master list.

EXPLANATION OF THE MASTER LIST
THE BIBLE

This copy of a master list is the music editors copy. It differs from the composer's copy only by the handwritten information. The written numbers to the left of the typewritten cue numbers refer to the footage in the reel where the cue starts. The next information is the typed cue number—then the recording information (picture — wild — etc.). This indicates the manner in which the cue will be recorded. Notice the click track information after those cues in which clicks are involved-24-0 clicks, 17.7 clicks, etc. Then the next information is the total time of the cue from the start of the first note to the start of the last note.

Six copies of this detailed master list are made and everyone pertinent to the recording session gets a copy. The dummy operator gets a copy so he can have the click or dialogue track ready. The projectionist has a copy to tell him how far in the reel he must wind down to start the picture cue. The recordist has a copy so he can tell how long the cue will run and be able to load his machine with enough tape to cover the recording of the cue. The composer uses his master list to check off the cues as he finishes them and makes sure that he has prepared all of the music for the recording, and finally, the copyist uses his bible as a check point to be sure that all of the music is finished and copied for the recording date.

The master list is a most valuable piece of information for every one concerned and most aptly named, "The Bible".

See glossary

EXAMPLE #12

I SPY #43

"TONIA"
MASTER MUSIC LIST

FOOTAGE
IN REEL   R-1

15'   M-11   PLAY IN PICTURE   :29

      M-12   PLAY OFF WILD   :06

337' M-13   PLAY IN PICTURE   :36

459' M-14   PICTURE *Special Cly -(opt)*   1:33 1/2

      R-2

10'   M-21   PICTURE   :16 2/3

35'   M-22   SOURCE PICTURE *17.7 CLX*   1:15 1/3

      M-23   PLAY IN   1:10

380' M-24   PICTURE   1:40 2/3

627' M-25   PICTURE   *24.0 CLX*   :48

696' M-26/31 PICTURE *Special Cly (opt)*   3:45 2/3

R3 AKID start →M26/31 A *Pict.*

      R-3/31 A

160' M-32   SOURCE PICTURE   1:28

292' M-33   PLAY OFF PICTURE   :18 1/2

345' M-34   PLAY IN PICTURE   :37

658' M-35   PICTURE   :43 1/2

      R-4

391' M-41   PICTURE   1:06 2/3

776' M-42   PLAY OFF PICTURE *9.6 Cly.*   1:21

      R-5

217' M-51   PICTURE   :32 1/3

      R-6

117' M-61   PICTURE   1:27 2/3

302' M-62   PLAY OFF PICTURE   :35

362' M-63   PLAY OFF PICTURE *9.1 Cly*   1:20 2/3

THE MECHANICS AND VOCABULARY
OF
FILM COMPOSITION

All of the examples are actual working cue sheets taken from films or T.V. shows. Most of them are from T.V., which offers a tremendous variety of mechanical procedures within the framework of a series. A feature film may have forty minutes, or more, of music in it. A T.V. series can have 28 episodes with as much as thirty minutes in each. As long as we accept the fact that the procedures are the same, T.V. gives us the widest area of useable examples.

*   *   *

As you read the cue through, you will get the story point. At the same time, you will be introduced to the abbreviations of everyday film language. The glossary of this book contains a complete set of the useable film abbreviations. (See Example #13, Page 42)

All timings are in seconds or parts of seconds. The start of each cue is indicated as :00 seconds.

*   *   *

At the start of the cue:

   :00 C.U. (close up)

:02 1/3 Cut to B.C.U. (big close up)

:04 Camera begins slowly panning to right. (This indicates a strong camera move and as you will see by studying the score, this feeling of movement was captured in the orchestra and kept its movement until camera stopped panning.)

:06 Tonia O.S. (Tonia is the girl's name in this episode, O.S. means off stage).

:46 Start Dissolve*

(a dissolve is one of many photographic optical effects that are used to denote the passage of time and/or place. The dissolve is a photographic device of the outgoing piece of film into the incoming. The visual effect is of one scene "bleeding" into another. The normal T.V. dissolve is 3 feet (2 seconds) although for special effects, we lengthen them up to 50 feet. These longer dissolves give you a superimposition effect that makes one scene seem to linger into another).

In order to begin the creative process, you have to first take stock of your principle picture obligations. You do this by circling the timings that are critical. If you will check the cue sheet, you will find that the following timings have been circled:

   :04, :12, :26 2/3rds, :45 1/3rd, and :48 seconds.

See glossary

THE BREAKDOWN OF A FILM

Because there was continuous dialogue and most of the critical timings fell on even seconds, a 24 frame click track seemed a good choice. One beat per second is practical for the dialogue burden and the bar breakdown is easy to lay out by yourself. **On the score of Example #13A, the numbers below the x's are click numbers—the circled numbers above are timings in seconds. This seems a good time** to bring up a point that will be reiterated many times in this book. THE FIRST CLICK OF ANY CLICK TRACK = :00 SECONDS. While this is an obvious statement, it is easy to forget. The first downbeat is always :00. If you examine the concert score you will see the click layout, the timings below, and the way that the music expresses what is essentially a warm conversation between two people into a moving shot implying menace. You will note that the movement started in the orchestra at the beginning of the pan shot at :04. This is a principle obligation to start the complete pattern of the cue. There is a set-in of sharp dissonance at 12 seconds to heighten the visual effect of seeing the wire. Just after the 26th second, (27th click) the bass starts to move into play to exaggerate the cut to the exterior. From a purely mathematical division of 1/2 of a 24 frame click, the bass part really entered at 26 1/2 seconds, but because the bass end of the orchestra speaks rather slowly the effect is late enough to give the feeling of :26-2/3rds seconds, the dead cue. The movements starts to trail off and comes to a hold just after the 46th click at :45-1/3rd seconds. The orchestra then holds long for a new cue. This is a very simple but effective use of a click track. Because it was a simple click, one beat per second, it was easy to lay out without having to have a bar breakdown made. One advantage of making your own breakdowns, when possible, is that the cutter will usually makes a breakdown to a fixed time signature. When you make your own, you can shift the bar line and time values at your own convenience.

I might point out that in the slower tempos, a beat can be subdivided into actual rhythmic values. Twenty-five and two-thirds seconds mathematically occurs on the third note of the eighth-note triplet after the twenty-seventh beat. Each note of a triplet value is worth eight frames in this tempo. However, with the entrance of the basses and the third horn at that point, a triplet would have more than likely "looked late." It would also have caused the cut to have more significance than it deserved because it would have created a noticeable lurch in the music which had been traveling in even eighths.

EXAMPLE #13

I SPY #43   647'

T1

M-25

Picture
Tonia has caught herself laughing at
Scott's mess with the oven. He, reflecting,
observes: "JUST REMEMBER - THOSE WHO CAN
LAUGH, CAN ALSO FEEL PAIN."

:00   Music Starts in the C.U. of Scott-just
             after his line.

:02 1/3   Cut to B.C.U. Tonia smiling (an expression
             she-up to now- has not often used.)

:04   Camera begins slowly panning down to right
             toward floor and base-board.

:06 2/3   Tonia, O.S. starts talking-quite pleasantly
             for a change: "YOU KNOW, I MUST ADMIT THAT
             YOU WERE RATHER IMPRESSIVE IN THE BAR
             TONIGHT." (Ends :12)

:12   The camera - still panning - reveals
             a microphone wire lying on floor and
             continues panning to follow it.

:13 2/3   Scott's voice, O.S.:   "AND I MUST ADMIT I
             WAS TERRIBLY, TERRIBLY FRIGHTENED."

:18 1/3   She starts a small protest in his favor: "NO,
             YOU SHOWED COURAGE, WHAT YOU SAID HAD MERIT
             EVEN THOUGH I DISAGREE WITH YOUR...PHILOSOPHIA."
             (Ends :26 1/3)

:26 2/3   Cut to exterior showing the sinister looking
             wire leading out over window ledge. The camera
             still following it stealthily.

:27 1/3   Scott's voice O.S.:   "YEAH, WELL I FIGURED
             YOU'D DO THAT." (Ends :29) Camera continues
             to follow wire hanging down outside wall of
             the tenement building.

:30 1/3   Tonia, O.S. resumes: "PERHAPS IT WOULD BE
             VALUABLE TO KNOW YOU BETTER-AH-IT WOULD
             SHARPEN MY OWN CONVICTIONS. "Scott agrees:
             "YEAH, I THINK SO." She continues: "THIS
             WOULD BE IN THE SPIRIT OF POLITICAL SCIENCE
             OF COURSE." Scott agrees: "OH YES, I'M IN
             FAVOR OF SCIENCE, I THINK IT'S A WONDERFUL
             THING-SCIENCE." (Ends :46 1/3)

Ed. Note (THE NOTATION T1) INDICATES THAT
TAKE #1 IS THE ACCEPTED TAKE

EXAMPLE #13 (Cont.)

I SPY #43

M-25 (P. 2.)

:33 1/3   Cut to interior of C.U. window sill-showing
               the wire coming into a room. (NOTE: The
               previous lines of dialogue are continuous, and
               overlap this cut as camera continues panning
               wire.)

:44   At this point the camera reveals wire leading
               to a tape recorder in operation on a table.

:45 1/3   Camera stops panning - centered on recorder.

:46   Start Dissolve.

:48   Music Ends as picture Full-In on high angle
               view of broad street & large buildings.

               (NOTE: Seques to Cue M-26/31)

TOTAL TIME :48

EXAMPLE #13A

TITLE _"THE WIRE"_ Page ①

Prod. _"I SPY" #43_ Cue _M-25 (CONCERT SCORE)_ Comp. _EARLE HAGEN_

Record Band #1

EXAMPLE #13A (Cont.)

TITLE _____

Prod. _____   Cue _____   Comp. _____

EXAMPLE #13A (Cont.)

TITLE _____ Page ③

Prod. _____ Cue _____ Comp. _____

Example #14 is the cue that followed the one we have just analyzed in this particular picture. It presents some interesting problems and some simple solutions. In this cue, M26/31, (the two reel numbers mean that this cue started in reel two and crossed over to reel three) we start with an Overlap* from the preceding cue. The term "overlap" means that this cue starts as the outgoing cue holds. The explanation of how these problems are handled in Dubbing* will come later in this book when we describe the final processes in film music. If you examine the last chord in M25, you will see that the structure which is held is a three part chord spelling down: A natural, F sharp, and A sharp. The overlap segue is indicated at the end of M25 by, "overlap M26/31". Actually, the last chord of M25 is held long and is lost under the start of M26/31 which starts with a fluctuating pattern that moves back and forth from A to B flat and then resolves from A to B natural. The A to B flat figure at the start of M26/31 matches the tonality of the outgoing chord, A, F sharp, A sharp, and when finally put together sounds like a continuation of the cue. This matter of overlaps is a major part of the mechanics. We use the overlap all of the time. Whenever there is a very long cue that can be broken into smaller segments for reasons of changes in key or character, or for the simple expediency of reducing the recording and playing problems on the stage, look for overlaps.

If you examine the cue sheets of Example #14, you will see that the scene is quite different in character than M25. It starts with a scenic setting and is gay and bright in character. The music in mind was relatively bright in tempo and a 9 frame click seemed to be the right speed. Once again, this is a self-constructed layout. Once again, the critical timings were circled. While these were really not obligatory, leaning on cuts of your principle characters gives the music a personalized feel that marries it to your picture. If you can find ways to catch principle cuts within the framework of a natural musical approach, you are always ahead. At no time should you sacrifice musical continuity to catch relatively unimportant cuts. The trick is to do it inside the natural flow of the music in such a way as to be part of the music itself. The layout for this kind of cue is a little more complicated and involves some simple mathematics. After you have circled your principle timings, you want to find the number of the click that will catch that timing. This is done by converting your timing to frames and dividing the total amount of frames by your click track unit. To this figure you must <u>add one click</u> for the zero timing. We will start with the first principle timing: 14 seconds.

$$
\begin{array}{r}
14 \text{ sec.} \\
\underline{24} \text{ frms.} \\
56 \\
\underline{28} \\
336 \text{ frms.}
\end{array}
$$

336 frms. ÷ 9 frm. clk. trk.

$$
\begin{array}{r}
37 \\
9\overline{)336} \quad \text{37+ or 38− (add 1 clk.) 38+ or 39−} \\
\underline{27} \\
66 \\
\underline{63} \\
3
\end{array}
$$

*See glossary

                                    I SPY #43   716'

Opt. Spec C4 (9FREE)

M-26/31 (NOTE: SEGUES FROM CUE M-25)

T4

:00	Music Starts at start of dissolve from a C.U. of tape recorder on a table as it records dialogue of Tonia & Scott from her apartment several floors above.
:02	Full In on high-angle view of broad street and large buildings.
:03	Camera begins tilting slowly down to bring in a very broad balustraded landing area of the Spanish Steps.
:12 1/3	Camera stops tilting as we see a small vendor's pie cart with parasol.

C4 #39' :14 — Cut to M.S. of Tonia's pie cart. She is selling to a man and woman—a couple of tourists.

:19 — Tonia casts a look to her rear-past camera L.

:19 1/3 — Cut to M.L.S. Scott seated with a newspaper atop a corner of the balustrade.

C4 #56 :20 1/2 — Cut to C.U. Scott

:21 2/3 — He raises newspaper as he looks back at Tonia as in giving her a greeting.

:22 2/3 — Cut to C.U. Tonia looking O.S. at Scott.

:23 — She turns back to face customers as the woman customer O.S. says: " GO AHEAD, BUDDY, AND TRY IT. " (Ends :25 1/3)

:25 2/3 — Cut to Three-Shot, Tonia, and her two customers.

:26 2/3 — The man picks up one of the pies as though he'd never seen anything like it before.

:27 1/3 — He chomps into it bravely.

:28 — Woman says: " HE'S A REAL CUTIE, MY HUSBAND, IF HE DON'T LIKE IT, HE'LL TELL YOU."(Ends :31)

:31 1/3 — Cut to C.U. Tonia awaiting the verdict on her pies.

:33 — Cut to close Two-Shot – the man chewing away at pie as a gradual look of approval comes over his face.

:34 2/3 — He says to wife: " IT'S DELICIOUS."(Ends :35 1/2)

:36 — Cut to C.U. Tonia greatly relieved & pleased.

:37 2/3 — Cut back to man and wife.

(cont'd.)

EXAMPLE #14 (Cont.)

I SPY #43

M-26/31 (P. 2.)

:38 1/3   Wife. embarrassed: " DON'T STUFF YOUR FACE IN PUBLIC, FOR HEAVEN'S SAKE." Wife to Tonia: " WE'LL TAKE HALF A DOZEN---." (Ends :44 2/3)

:45   Cut to C.U. Tonia as she starts putting pies in bag.

:47 2/3   Cut to C.U. Scott-still watching.

:49 2/3   He takes off his dark glasses to see better.

:50 2/3   Cut to Tonia finishing putting pies in bag.

:54   Tonia: " GRAZIA. " Woman: " PREGO. " Man: " MOLTO GOOD." (Ends :56 1/2)

:58 1/3   Man and wife exit as Tonia casts glance back at Scott.

:59   Cut to M.L.S. Scott on balustrade.

1:00 1/3   He jumps down and starts running toward Tonia.

1:03   As he reaches to happily embrace Tonia, he says: " NOW." NOW." WHAT DO YOU THINK OF THAT." HAH? I ASK YOU DID MY MAN---TASTE HIMSELF SOME GENUINE ITALIAN CAKES, OR, DID HE NOT? "

1:11 2/3   She answers: " NO, HE HAD SOME PHILADELPHIA---"

1:15 1/3   He breaks in: " LOOK, DON'T RUIN THE MAN'S HOME MOVIES, NOW LISTEN 'TIL I ASK YOU A QUESTION, ARE WE GOING TO REST ON OUR LAURELS?" (End 1:20 1/3)

1:20 1/3   Cut to C.U. Tonia.

1:20 1/2   She says: "NO. " (Ends 1:20 2/3)

1:21 1/3   He, O.S.: " OH YES WE ARE, I'M QUITTING WHILE I'M AHEAD BECAUSE I'M AFRAID THE TENSION IS TOO MUCH FOR ME. " (Ends 1:26 2/3)

1:22 1/3   Cut to C.U. Scott reaching into his pocket for some money. (NOTE: Previous line overlaps.)

1:26 2/3   Cut to Full Shot as the two continue in a good natured argument. She protests as he puts money in her pocket: "AH." NOW VOGLIO." He says: "WE ARE GOING ON A PICNIC, HERE WE GO-OFF ON A PICNIC." (Ends 1:34 1/3)

1:34 1/3   Cut to C.U. Tonia-protesting futilely.

(cont'd.)

EXAMPLE #14A

Record Band #1

EXAMPLE #14A (Cont.)

Prod. _____   Title _____   Page ___

The click number is indicated to the left of the cue sheet timing as click #39⁻ (minus). Notice in the score the run up to the 39th click to absorb the minus factor. In a tempo as fast as a 9 frame click, runs, appoggiaturas, or grace notes can be used to take up minute variations in clicks. It is better to be slightly behind the cut than ahead. By the time the eye has absorbed the cut, the music has set.

The second principle timing — :20 1/2 secs. is handled the same way. The seconds are converted to frames and divided by the click track unit.

$$20 \ (1/2)$$
$$\underline{24}$$
$$80$$
$$\underline{40}$$
$$480$$

$$480 + 1/2 \ (12 \text{ frms.}) = 492 \div 9$$

$\quad 54$	$54+ \ \ 55-$
$9\overline{)492}$	
$\underline{\ \ 45}$	Add 1 clk.
$\ \ 42$	$55+$ or $56-$
$\ \ \underline{36}$	
$\ \ \ 6$	

One click is added for zero — :00 and the click number is indicated as 55+ or 56—. Inasmuch as it appears as a repeat phrase in the music, the downbeat of 56— was used and once again, the grace notes take up the slack between the 55th clk. and the 56th clk.

If you are going to work with click tracks, you might as well get used to the decimal system for click tracks that deal with 1/2 holes. Each 1/2 hole of any click is = .125 sec. That means that you would translate click tracks as follows:

7 frm. clk. = 7 frms.
7-1 clk   = 7.125
7-2 cls.   = 7.250
7-3 clk.   = 7.375
7-4 clk.   = 7.500
7-5 clk.   = 7,625
7-6 clk.   = 7.750
7-7 clk.   = 7.875

These decimal designations hold for all click tracks.

A 10-3 click would be decimalized as 10.375.

To illustrate, let us take the following example:
Given a 7-2 click track, find out at what beat (+ or —) 43 seconds happens.

```
Convert      43  sec.
             24  frms.
            ———
            172
             86
            ————
           1032  frms.


             142
      ————————————
7250 / 1032000      = 142+ — add 1 beat for :00 and the
       7250
      ————
      30700          answer is 143+
      29000
      ————
      17000
      14500
      ————
        500
```

You can use this decimal system whenever necessary. There will be more about this in the chapter on conversions.

If you were working with a slower click track, you could actually divide the fractions left over in converting into musical time values. For example, in a 24 frame click track a fraction of 16/24ths (1/3) left over from a click number would be the third note of a triplet.

To arrive at the rest of the click track numbers repeat this same process. Multiply the timing by 24 convert to frames and divide by the click track unit. This will locate the beat on which the specific timing will fall. It is a good idea to convert all of the timings in which you are interested into click numbers before starting to lay out the music. In this cue, you will notice that to get the musical phrases to fall on the downbeats, (desireable in this case as opposed to the previous example where cues were caught on and off of the beats), there is a great deal of time value changes and bar line shifting. The score starts in 3/4 for 2 bars, goes to 4/4 through bar 13, then shifts to 5/4 to pick up an extra beat in order to land on the repeat musical phrase on the 56th beat. This example has been continued a ways to illustrate another trick that can be handled with clicks. Bar 17 is in 4/4, bar 18 in 3/4, and bar 19 is in 6/8. There are 2 clicks to this 6/8 bar, but because the eighth note is l'istesso, the distance between these two clicks had to be 1 1/2 times longer to allow for the extra eighth note per click. Clicks #71 and #72 have 4 1/2 frames added to them. The mathematical distance between the clicks is exactly correct and the click track matches the time value exactly. In the bar following, two quarter notes lead to a duet which starts on the down beat of bar 21. This is an example of pure musical expression clicked out. The orchestra sailed through the 6/8 bar without the slightest hitch and the musical effect was achieved. This example has been used to point out, once again, that the click track can give you freedom in your writing concept if you understand how to make clicks work for you.

One of the problems of click tracks is that as the music is being played, the feeling of tempo is strongly felt. If it is your purpose to present the feeling of tempo, well and good. However, if musically you do not desire the tempo to be felt, but you are using the click track as an expediency to catch critical timings, then you must investigate the ways to destroy the feeling of pulse. Rhythmic supensions across the bar line, quarter note triplets, long notes of uneven values, written rubatos, and such other devices can be employed to break the feeling of tempo. A click track can be a definite attribute when you want the feeling of pulse without writing it in the orchestra. Feeding a click to a group of strings to have them play with a feeling of pulse is a constantly used device. The rhythmic implication can be most definitely felt in the performance.

The above example of dividing the amounts of values of the normal click track itself opens a whole field that to the best of my knowledge is virtually untapped. Frankly, I don't believe that too much experimentation has been made in this area and that the possibilities are unlimited. One of the most common complaints of the composer is that when he has to work to click tracks, his musical expression is necessarily limited by the metronomic nature of the click beat. It is possible with the building of special click tracks to give the composer tremendous freedom of expression rhythmically. The problem is that these special tracks must be worked out by the composer as he writes the music. It becomes his responsibility not only to devise these special tracks to conform to his music, but also to make a foolproof layout indicating the exact amount of frames for each beat so that the music cutter can build these special click tracks. This subject will be covered at the end of the section on click tracks.

Decimalization of click tracks are the standard in the industry. Before the pocket calculator became a drugstore item, there was some heavy math involved in being accurate. With the calculator sitting on your desk or the podium, the math is duck soup. Unfortunately, being accurate is a personal habit — one that requires very little extra effort. It is a total mystery to me why some composers are content in just being "close" to a dramatic requirement. When :08 of a second is your limit of error, "close" isn't good enough. Besides, with a five-dollar calculator you can nail any cue "dead-on" anywhere you wish. It's easy.

CHAPTER 6
CONVERSIONS

Let us assume that you have a timing in mind that you want to meet. You have laid out a rough musical phrase to the point where the critical timing occurs. You know how many beats are involved and you would like to find the number of the click that will nail the cue dead. Let us say that the critical timing is :22 1/2 seconds. Your musical tempo is somewhere around 142 to 146 on the metronome. Let me caution you at this point that no metronome is accurate. Use it as a rough guide and check your timings with a stopwatch and the click track chart. The musical phrase you have in mind has 55 beats in it, the 55th beat being the down beat that you wish to hit. How do you find the proper click track unit?

The method for doing this is once again by conversion. Convert your seconds to frames. :22.5 seconds x 24 frames = 540 frames. Now divide by the number of beats you need—BUT!!!—remember that the first click of any click track equals :00!! That means that whenever you work this kind of problem you must subtract the first click from the total number you need. You are dealing with lapsed time only. Subtract the first click from the 55 you are looking for and divide 54 beats into 540 frames. The answer is a 10 frame click track.

Let's take a slightly more complicated example. You wish to hit a timing of :26-1/3rd seconds on the 33rd click. The same mathematical process brings you into a fractional click. :26-1/3 converted to frames equals 632 frames. Drop the first beat and divide 32 into 632. You get an answer of 19 and 24/32. Reduce the fraction 24/32 to eights, the number of 1/2 holes in a frame and you get 6/8ths. The answer is a 19-6 click.

26   1/3 sec. in 32 beats
26   1/3 x 24 frms. = 632 frms.

$$\begin{array}{r} 19 \\ 32\overline{)632} \\ 32 \\ \hline 312 \\ 288 \\ \hline 24 \end{array}$$

19 24/32—Reduce 24/32 to 6/8

19 — 6 clk. trk.

When you are working to find the click track, remember to <u>drop</u> the first beat in your figuring and always reduce the fractions to the nearest eighth.

Sometimes it is not possible to reduce the fractions to 8ths. In that case adjust the fraction so that it can be reduced to 8ths. Be sure and check these and all other clicks against picture before bringing them on the recording stage. An example of an answer that can not be reduced to eighths would be: 31 seconds in 27 beats. 31 seconds x 24 frames = 744 frames. If you drop the first beat and divide 744 by 26, you get an answer of 28-16/26ths. You can't reduce 16/26ths to 8ths, so you make a minor adjustment that you can reduce and change 16/26ths to 15/24. This can be reduced to 8ths, and your answer is a 28-5 click track. The actual computer count of the 27th beat of a 28-5 click track is :31.02. Each frame of picture is .04 (hundredths) of a second. Your answer is correct to the 1/2 frame of picture. Not too bad to play 27 beats of music in 31 seconds and only be .02 of a second off.

What if you did not want to be long by .02 of a second. Ridiculous, but it opens up the subject of variables. If you insist on losing the .02, you can instruct your cutter to subtract 1/2 hole of his punches every other beat for the last eight beats; this picks up the .02. Actually, there are many ways to add or lose 1/2 holes over a period of time and as long as the change is gradual, the orchestra won't even feel it. 1/2 hole subtracted every other beat accelerates the track .005 every other beat. This is a pretty far out example of a variable click track as you can imagine, and totally unnecessary in this instance. There are many cases, however, where variable click tracks are not only useful, but absolutely necessary.

Taking the same example and working it out in the decimal system would give us the following answer:

33 — 1 beat for :00 = 32 beats	19.750 clk.	19.750 clk. = 19-6 clk. trk.
26 1/3 sec. x 24 frms. = 632 frms.	32) 632	

$$
\begin{array}{r}
19.750 \\
32\overline{)632} \\
\underline{32} \\
312 \\
\underline{288} \\
240 \\
\underline{224} \\
160 \\
\underline{160} \\
000
\end{array}
$$

You can work these conversions by the eighth system or the decimal system. The decimal system is more accurate but a little more tedious. Either method will give you the right result. Once again, if you were to wind up with a decimal figure that was not exactly to the .125th of a second, you would have to go to the nearest equivalent. For example: an answer of 12.235 would indicate that the click was nearest to 12.250, (12-2) an answer of 23.800 would be interpreted as 23.750 (23-6). By the same reasoning, an answer that split the amount left over could be taken either way. 23.812 could indicate either 23-6 or 23-7.

THE MECHANICS AND VOCABULARY
OF
FILM COMPOSITION

EXERCISES AND SELF-ANALYSIS OF THE PRIMARY FUNCTION OF CLICKS

Devise for yourself a group of exercises that allow you to set a click tempo and locate the proper beat for a specific timing.

Example: The tempo desired is a 10 frame click track. 4 bars of 4/4 = 6.7 seconds. The desired timing is one minute and one and two thirds of a second, 1:01 and 2/3rds.

1. Convert seconds to frames. 61-2/3 x 24 = 1480 frames.

2. Divide frames by the click track unit.
   1480 ÷ 10 (frms) = 148.

3. Add one beat for the downbeat (:00).

4. The answer is 149 beats of a 10 frame click track.

By using the conversion method of changing seconds to frames you can solve any of the problems that you set up for yourself.

Keep in mind that when you are working to find a specific beat, you must <u>add</u> 1 beat for :00.

Keep in mind that when you are looking for lapsed time, you must <u>subtract</u> 1 beat for :00.

Another form of exercise is to lay out a melodic plan to bars of varying time values. Give yourself a specific time to catch. Number the total beats and find the click track.

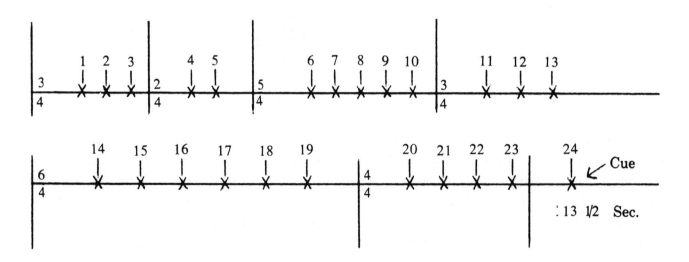

(14-1 clk. trk.)

Perhaps an easier way to remember when to add or subtract a beat is: If you know how many beats there are, subtract one. If you don't, add one.

CHAPTER 7
THE VARIABLE CLICK TRACK

In the first chapter of this book a statement was made that a cue could be caught to within 1/384th of a second. 1/2 hole is 1/192 of a second so in order to split the timing in half, we go to a variable click track down as an Alternating Click*. All this means is that to get into smaller fractions we alternate beats between two clicks. A 10-1 and 10-2 click track that alternates beat to beat gives us in effect a 10-1½ click. This would divide our fractions in half and provide us with timings down to 1/384th of a second. The real purpose of variables can be explained much more clearly if we go back to our original band dance cue in Chapter 4 and take a different problem. (See page 26 et seq.)

Let us suppose that when you were trying loops to find the proper tempo you fixed on the original 10-5 loop. Let us assume that the 10-5 loop held to picture synch for about 20 bars and then seemed to move ahead of the picture. This is a good indication that the dancers photographed were beginning to slow down. Don't forget that they were photographed with no audible music playing, because of dialogue recording, and the natural tendency is slow down. Assuming that they did slow down, we have to find out how much — and where. You run the picture down to the last eight bars and try loops at that point until you find the right tempo. For the sake of discussion, let's say that they slowed down to a 11-6 loop tempo. The original tempo of 10-5 has a metronome value of approximately 135. The 11-6 has a MM value of approximately 124. If you run a metronome at 135 and suddenly change it to 124, you will feel an enormous drop in tempo. Obviously, no dance band would make this sharp change of tempo in one bar; it would be extremely noticeable and annoying.

Let us assume two different kinds of problems in connection with this situation and find the resolution for each.

In the first situation, let's take the position that the slow down was gradual and took place over a period of 10 bars of 4/4 dance tempo. We have 40 beats in which we must add 9 1/2 holes to retard the track from a 10-5 to a 11-6 click. To make a smooth transition, we can add 1/2 hole on the down-beat of each bar for the last 9 bars. This very slight retardation will not be felt, either by the orchestra or the audience, and will bring you into the 11-6 click tempo at the desired place with practically no noticeable difference in the overall tempo. Once you work into the 11-6, you can continue this click to the end.

See glossary

In the second situation, let us assume that the change of tempo takes place immediately on a direct cut in the film. This is very common and indicates that a portion of the film was edited out during the time the dancers were slowing down. You are left with a visual dance track that goes directly from one tempo to another. As previously stated, an orchestra can not make this kind of change without lurching. In this case we have to cheat the tempo change and make the change as fast as is practical. We can take two bars on each side of the cut and spread our 1/2 hole additions on every other beat until the 9 1/2 holes are added to take you from the 10-5 click to the 11-6 click. The change of tempo is naturally more drastic, but because the 1/2 holes are added evenly, the retard is fairly smooth. Visually, the dancers seem to drift for a few bars and then lock in. If you have a relatively crowded floor of dancers, you probably won't even notice the visual change. On a crowded floor there is always an assortment of tempos going on. This helps mask the problem. If there are few dancers and their rhythm is pretty well locked together, you will have to settle for the short drift while you are making the tempo change. This situation should not happen, but often does. If you are engaged before the picture starts shooting, it will be your responsibility to see that it does not happen.

There are many other situations where a variable click is the only solution. Almost always they are imposed upon the composer by faulty procedures on the shooting stage. You have to take them as they come and handle them in as smooth a manner as possible. Working with minute tempo changes over the longest spread possible is the best solution.

There are times when tempos are so faulty that you can not work a loop to them at all. This calls for a Film Tapping* procedure. With the Moviola running at speed, take a white grease pencil and tap a piece of blank leader that is threaded up in the mag head. Tap out the tempo that you see. At the end of the sequence, you will have a visual white click tapped out on the leader. Measure the distance between the white marks and try to determine some pattern of tempo. This method always requires smoothing out. If you can determine a tempo that is a compromise and satisfies much of your picture obligation, start with that. If there are drastic changes that have to be met, you may have to resort to making the cue in short pieces with several overlaps. It is a fact that anything, anything whatsoever, can be matched if you use the full range of mechanical facilities at your disposal. Make up your mind that if you run into awkward situations, you are going to have to put in a lot of time at the Moviola with a batch of loops in hand.

ANALYSIS

The variable click track is never used electively. It is a poor means of retarding or accelerating tempo. Its use is always in the area of desperation and dictated solely by enforced picture commitments. There is no reason to exercise or develop any special technique in the area of variable clicks.

*See glossary

CHAPTER 8

SPECIAL CLICK TRACKS DESIGNED FOR CREATIVE EXPRESSION

In Example #14 we touched upon the subject of special click tracks. These tracks widen the latitude of expression for the composer, hold the orchestra together, and at the same time meet specific picture obligations. (See page 48).

If you will refer back to Example #12 (See page 39) you will notice that on the master list, M26/31 is listed as a special click track. This means that something out of the ordinary was designed by the composer and that a straight 9 frame click would not work. The change of time value, necessitating a change in the value of the clicks in bar 19 has been explained in detail on page 53. This slight change of rhythmic value was strictly for the aesthetic satisfaction of the composer and did not disturb in any way the obligations that he wanted to catch.

A much more sophisticated example of how click tracks can be built to give the composer freedom follows. Example #15 is a complicated click track layout. It involves changing bar lines, alla breve time values, shifts in clicks and many picture obligations. Although there are changes in the values of the clicks from bar to bar — bars 19, 20, 21, etc. — this is _not_ a variable click track. The basic time value remains the same throughout. All variations in tempo come off of the basic unit.

THE MECHANICS AND VOCABULARY
OF
FILM COMPOSITION

EXAMPLE #15

Special layout for clicks to match music. This information is to enable the cutter to build the special unit.

EXAMPLE #15

63

"I SPY" #76
(SPECIAL CLK TK) "OOPS, THE TROOPS" M23   EARLE HAGEN

EXAMPLE #15 (Cont.)

65

THE MECHANICS AND VOCABULARY
OF
FILM COMPOSITION

EXAMPLE #15A

The orchestrated sketch of the previous layout. The very sparse sketch was used both as a clix reference for the cutter and as a thin musical layout from which to orchestrate.

EXAMPLE #15A (Cont.)

EXAMPLE #15A (Cont.)

As notated on the top of the layout, the basic unit is a 12 frame click track in 4/4. The basic time unit is one beat (12 frames) per quarter note. Through the 5/4 bar at bar 8, through the 4/4 at bar 9, through the 3/4 at bar 13 and 14, the basic beat remains at one beat per quarter note. At bar 15, the time changes to a l'istesso ₵ (cut time). At this point we go to 2 clicks per bar and the value doubles to two quarter notes per beat. At bar 19 the time changes to 6/16. In order to stay constant with the relationship to our basic unit (12 frames), each click in the 6/16 bar is worth 3/4 of the original click value.

In 4/4 ⅄ (clk — 12 frms)	=	♩
In ₵ ⅄	=	½ ♩
In 2/4 ⅄	=	♩
1/2 ⅄ (6 frms)	=	♪
1/4 ⅄ (3 frms)	=	♬
3/16	=	¾ of original value (12 frms)
3/16	=	9 frms = ♪.

Because the 6/16 bar is conducted in 2, the track must be built so that the two beats in bar 19 have a value of 9 frames each. (3/4 of the value of the original click). The tempo in this bar is *faster*. The next bar, 20 is in 2/4 and has 2 beats of the original 12 frame unit — bar 21 is back to two 9 frame clicks — bar 22 and 23, 12 frame clicks — bar 24, 9 frame clicks — and so on. While the tempo jumps to a faster beat in the 6/16 bars, the music was created to produce that effect — or perhaps it would be more accurate to say that the track was built to implement the desired musical effect. This is totally different than a variable click track where the musical intent remains basically the same while the tracks are speeded up or slowed down to meet picture requirements.

In this example, the only qualification for the variation in time value was the desired musical effect on the part of the composer.

You will notice that the clicks are very carefully numbered — in sequence according to their accumulative amount. You will also notice that the end of the cue was on click #109½ — the exact number necessary to come out right for the end of the cue.

SPECIAL CLICK TRACKS DESIGNED
FOR CREATIVE EXPRESSION

The reason for the very detailed click track breakdown is to let the music cutter know exactly what you want. This differs from the bar breakdown where the cutter gives the composer the action in detail. In this case the cutter can not even begin to prepare the sequence until the composer gives him the exact information that is needed. In this way, and only in this way, you can be sure that when you walk on the stage to record, the click track will match the music. It is not a bad idea to go into the studio and run the click track against the sketch layout to make sure that the two do match. Any precaution that you can take prior to recording can save you time and money and help make the end result better. The control of the medium is at all times the responsibility of the composer and he must not assume that anyone can tell what he has in mind. This kind of special click track may only match the picture in a general way. Its primary purpose may be to help keep the orchestra together through unusual time changes, and as far as the pictures goes, to start and stop at the right places. Keep in mind that generally the time you will have to rehearse is limited. Add to that the fact that the orchestra will be spread out all over the recording stage and you have a set-up for confusion. The trumpet player on one side of the stage will hear the pop of the click precisely at the same time as the percussionist at the other side of the stage. The judicious use of a click can definitely help keep them together.

The very sparse sketch is sufficient for the music cutter to start building the special click while you proceed to orchestrate the cue. Generally a photostat or thermofax of the original will allow each of you to have a copy and proceed on your separate ways. I have illustrated this example with the click track layout and a reduction of the orchestrated score.

Before we leave the section on click tracks, it should be mentioned that there is a short cut to finding the approximate click that you will need. With the metronome set at the approximate tempo, start your watch on the first count, count to 24 and stop the watch on the 25th beat. Translate this into frames instead of seconds and you should have the approximate click with which to start. Example: The 25th beat is 10 1/2 seconds. You would be in the tempo of a 10 1/2 frame click track (10-4). This is approximate. By working with the stop watch, loops, and/or the exact timings needed, you can pinpoint the exact click desired. This short cut method only serves to give you a starting point.

By now you should have a pretty fair knowledge of what click tracks are about. You have also been introduced into the film language. We shall continue to build that language as we proceed.

THE MECHANICS AND VOCABULARY
OF
FILM COMPOSITION

CHAPTER 9
THE MECHANICS OF FREE TIMING

The other basic ways to record for films are called Free Timing*. The two most common methods are stopwatch and picture cueing.

The most common form of film recording is done to stopwatch. The type of stop watch can be the pocket variety or the studio stop clock pictured in Example #16. It is most certainly advisable to invest in a good stopwatch. The most practical kind is also pictured in Example # 16 A, and has two second hands that are independently controlled. You can stop one hand while the other is running. This is invaluable for checking inside cues while you are conducting. All of your writing, except for bar breakdowns, will involve the stopwatch, so by all means get the best one you can afford. Stopwatches can be purchased for $7.00 to $85.00. The large studio clocks are great for conducting. Usually, if you have a cutter working with you, the cutter will start the clock, on cue, from a remote switch. This is very helpful to the conductor as it frees his left hand.

The luxury and convenience of picture recording is not generally used throughout the many facets of the film music industry. Most operations prefer to sacrifice quality and cut costs by recording Wild*, (without picture), and depend on cutting and trimming the music after recording to make it fit. The whole Track* industry is based on wild recording. Of necessity, track, to be useable, must not and cannot be pertinent to any specific film needs. It is usually lumped together under headings and classifications such as: "Dramatic", "Heavy Dramatic", "Comedy", "Chase", "Fight", etc. To my way of thinking, the very impersonal nature of track defeats its purpose as film music. It can operate on only the most general of terms and becomes so much wallpaper as far as real emotional value is concerned. Still and all, it remains a large industry and many fine composers have written music for it. Industrial films, commercials, and many T.V. companies record track, or in the manner of track. They record only to clicks and stopwatch and never play any music back during the recording session.

See glossary

EXAMPLE #16   Studio Stop Clock

EXAMPLE #16A   Pocket Stop Watch

Two Second Hands, Dual Controlled Fifth-second Timer

Regardless of the methods or the reasons implied, the composers handling of the stopwatch is the single most important phase in the film writing technique. Of course, this book excludes the music itself. Music and composition are not the purpose behind this book.

When you write to a cue sheet, be sure that you *hear* the orchestra accurately. Always time the phrases as you hear them being played. That means that if a musical phrase is written with a rubato in mind, the time that is occupied by the rubato must be accounted for on the stopwatch. This is absolutely necessary if you are to get the performance you desire and still meet your timing requirements. If you are not recording to picture, it is helpful to notate on the score where the principal points of action fall. See Ex. 17A. This helps you keep in mind the picture action without having to refer to the cue sheet. Be assured that when you conduct your own scores to stopwatch, you will be very busy indeed.

Between watching the stopwatch for your timings, keeping one eye on the score for tempo and time value changes and conducting, you should have your hands full.

Never, and that means *NEVER*, squeeze your music. If you are writing to stopwatch and you cannot get a musical phrase to come out naturally without rushing it or Squeezing* it, change the phrase. Try to find a shift in the bar line to pick up the time you need. Try to change 4/4 bar to 3/4, or two 3/4 bars to 5/4 rather than rush to make a timing. You will find that you can develop the facility to diminish or augment time values easily to pick up or lose time. It can be done without hurting the music at all if you apply yourself to think of the bar lines as being fluid. We say about the good picture composers that you can "fall through" their timings. This means that they have become so adept at writing naturally for timings that the musical phrases, concept, and orchestration almost prohibit you from playing the music any way but right.

The natural tendency for a composer starting out in films is to overwrite. Too much music, and not enough time to say it. The real masters of the film technique are usually understating what they have to say. They have, through experience, come to the full realization that the picture business, whether it be movies, T.V., commercials, or industrials, is essentially a visual medium and that a little bit of the right music in the right place goes a long way. Unlike the concert hall or recordings, where the medium is aural, in film music the obligation to change color frequently, orchestrate floridly, and to try to say it all with music is not only unnecessary, but in many cases completely undesireable. This is not to say that the music has to be banal. On the contrary, there is plenty of opportunity to express yourself. What you must learn to recognize is at which time does the music really "carry the ball". When that moment occurs, you can go all out. Until those moments do occur, you might as well accept the fact that music is an emotional adjunct to the film and write accordingly.

*See glossary

EXAMPLE #17

(T1)   I SPY #28   ST. MK   245'

M-12   PLAYOFF PICTURE   265 ft

(:00)   K is in taxi with Vanessa. As he starts to put on his shirt
          the driver suddenly clobbers him with blackjack. Music
          starts on the hit.

:00-2/3   K falls back against Van

:01   Cut CS, K as he falls unconscious

:02   Van o.s. "JUST RELAX KELLY DEAR" (:03-2/3)

(:04)   Cut MCS driver reaching in his pocket

:05   He pulls out hankershief with something wrapped in it

:06-1/2   He unwraps hyperdermic needle

:07-1/3   He holds it up

:08   He frees the air bubble

:09-1/3   He turns to back seat and starts to reach back with needle

:10-1/2   Cut to CS, K out cold
:10-2/3
:12-2/3   K's eyes flutter slightly

:13   Cut driver giving injection
:14
:16-2/3   He turns around again

:17-1/2   He places needle back in hankerchief

:17-2/3   Cut CS, K as Van o.s. "IT WOULD HAVE BEEN A CHARMING EVENING,
          KELLY" (:19-2/3)

:20-1/2   Van "BUT THE ONE WE HAVE PLANNED FOR YOU SHOULD BE EVEN
          MORE FUN" (:23-2/3)

:24-2/3   Cut MS taxi

:25-2/3   Taxi starts pull away

:27-2/3   Camera pans as cab starts by

:29   Cab going away from camera
:29-2/3
:33-2/3   First frame of Main Title

          TOTAL TIME :33-2/3

Prod. "I SPY" #28, M-12   Title   EXAMPLE #17 A

Composer *EARLE HAGEN*
Arranger   *Pg. 1.*

(NOTE:- EACH STRING ENTRANCE STARTS ON ¼ TONE BEND.)

Prod. _____   Title   **EXAMPLE #17 A (Cont.)**   Composer _____

Arranger   *Pg. 2*

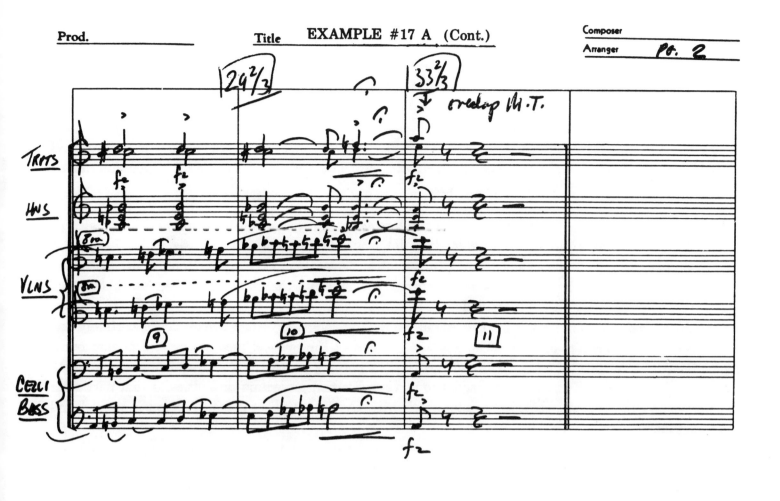

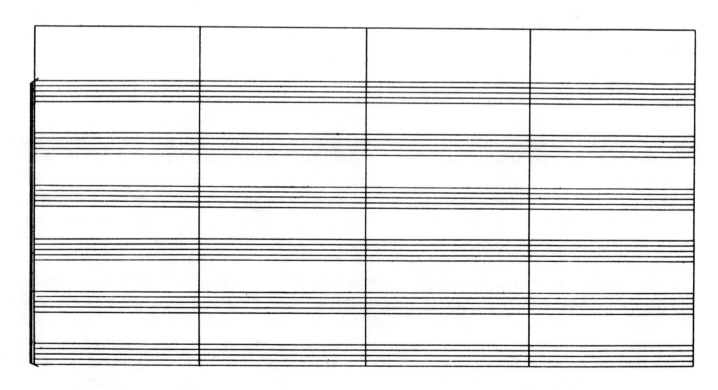

THE MECHANICS AND VOCABULARY
OF
FILM COMPOSITION

The more experience you gain in writing, the less you will write. Your timings will become more and more natural; your orchestration will probably have less doublings; you will find yourself looking for tensions that create harmonic movement instead of rhythmic movement under dialogue. These are the film growing-pains that really catalyze your creativity and as you write you will discover that you can continuously increase your productivity with less and less means, and without sacrificing the musical integrity in which you believe.

There is no rule of thumb that can tell you how fast or how slow music should be under dialogue. If there were such a rule, it more often than not would be no faster than 1 second per beat. At 1 second per beat, the tendency is to want to put a lot of movement in the score. Don't do it! Leave the movement alone and look for lines and sonority. If you can write something effective that is still slower, you can't get hurt. Under dialogue, it is almost impossible to be too slow, but you can be much too fast. Example 18A is a good case in point. The composer, Hugo Friedhofer, is certainly one of the finest in the film industry. There is total control of the musical medium as well as film craft. Notice the total lack of panic in the orchestra. Yet nothing is lost in the way of musical interest. This cue was originally prepared to record to picture. We had projection difficulties at that particular moment so the cue was recorded to stopwatch with absolutely no problem. The music played and timed itself.

The stopwatch is the link between the creative process and the fulfillment on the recording stage. Get into the habit of starting and stopping your watch without looking at it while you time a phrase. Start your watch on the first note of the music; try to hear the orchestra playing your music, and then stop the watch at the end of the phrase. Then look at your watch and check your timing. If you are short or long, repeat the process. Try not to make any noticeable tempo adjustment. If the second time you try the timing process you are still too short or too long, the length of the musical phrase is wrong and has to be changed. Looking at the watch while you check your timings sets up a subconscious change in tempo to accommodate the timing you are trying to hit. Unless the music is extremely flexible and can be slowed down or speeded up without distorting it, you are better off to re-examine the musical phrase and shorten or lengthen it, whatever the case may be. When writing music to be conducted to a stopwatch, give yourself some kind of Safety Valve* before a dead cue. This safety valve can be a simple tenuto, a short hold, or a bar with no movement in the last half. Whatever you lose in the way of musical interest will be more than made up in practicability. If you are recording to stopwatch, there is more than likely a cost factor involved. This cost factor limits the time you have for rehearsal and recording. In the film recording business there is no time allowed for rehearsal. You pay straight recording time from the moment the musicians are called until the date is finished. If there is any complaint about the film music business, it is the appalling lack of time. Time to create; time to write, and time to record. The studio musicians are amongst the finest sight readers in the musical world. You must remember, however, that they will still be sight reading on the takes. Anything that you can do to eliminate confusion is to your own advantage. A bar that has to suddenly be rushed to catch a cue has a good chance of being missed. A sudden non-marked hold at the end of a bar with a lot of movement in it is a license for trouble.

*See glossary

EXAMPLE #18

I SPY #39

X-41 (P. 4) _SCORE STARTS HERE_
①1:24

| 1:24 2/3 | Cut back to Kelly & Kathy. (NOTE: Foregoing line overlaps this.) |

1:29 1/3   Kathy, rather sadly, continues: "BUT THE
⊕1:30   WORLD WOULDN'T HAVE THAT - NOT FOR VERY LONG."
              (Ends 1:31 1/3)

1:33 1/3   Kathy: "YOU SEE, DINO WAS MARRIED AS YOU
⊕ 1:36   SAID AND A, " (Ends 1:35 1/3)

1:37   Kathy cont: "THERE'S NO DIVORCE IN ITALY." (Ends 1:38 1/3)

1:40 2/3   Kathy cont: "MOTHER FINALLY DECIDED TO GO
（1:42）   HOME AND..."

1:42 1/3   An O.S. voice with Italian accent interrupts
              her: "MISS CARTWRIGHT," (Ends 1:43 2/3)

1:44   She looks up O.S.L. - not at first recognizing
              the person.

1:46   Cut to C.U. of a handsome Italian - smiling.

1:47 1/3   His smile starts to fade just slightly -
              apparently because he is not recognized.

⊕1:48   Cut to C.U. Kathy looking up O.S.L. and not
              quite believing her eyes.

1:50   She, breathlessly with surprise, says: "WELL,
              DINO! (Ends 1:51)

1:51 1/2   Cut back to C.U. of the handsome Italian.

1:52   He says: "I'M ALDO, DINO'S SON." (Ends 1:54 1/3)
⊕ 1:54
1:54 2/3   Cut to C.U. - Kathy - smitten.

1:56   She recovers sufficiently to give him a
              slight little glance of appraisal.

1:57 1/2   Cut to C.U. Kelly giving with the cynical scrutiny.

1:59 1/2   Cut to C.U. Scott - a little non-plused.

2:00 2/3   Scott makes a kind of "so what?" facial expression.
⊕2:01
2:02 1/2   Cut back to C.U. of Aldo - still waiting for
              something more of a reception.

2:03 1/2   Start to Fade-Out.

⊕（2:05）   Full Out to commercial (1/2 sec. allowed)

TOTAL TIME 2:05

(NOTE: NO "PLAY-IN")

Prod. _____ Title **EXAMPLE #18A** Composer *HUGO FRIEDHOFER*

("I SPY" #39-M-41) Arranger _____ ①

Prod. _____ Title **EXAMPLE #18A (Cont.)** Composer _____

Arranger _____

To plan out your timing, take the meat of a phrase and lay it out on a single line of a sketch. Let us suppose that the phrase is to last 10 seconds before you have a picture obligation. It is not necessary to sketch the music completely for a timing layout. After all, it is your music and you know who is going to play it. Let us further assume that the music is to be melodic. Take your single line layout and time it. Check it again. If it comes out right, sketch in your accompaniment making sure when you do that it will not change the speed of the music and alter the original timing. If your next obligation is at :23 1/3rd seconds, continue your single line sketch from :10 sec. to :23 1/3rd sec. You are now working on a :13 1/3rd sec. timing phrase. When you have that worked out, time the whole layout from the beginning, :00 to :23-1/3rd. If anywhere at all the music or the timing seems unnatural, check it again. If it still doesn't work, find the bar or bars that are giving you trouble and see if changing a bar line helps. Try to find a way to pick up or drop a beat without hurting the melodic line. Check it again from the top. If it works, proceed to the next critical timing. Each time you add a block of time to your layout, try to make the continuity flow *from the top*. Even though you may be building your overall cue in small blocks of time, you do not want it to sound episodic. If the scene and the music are supposed to be episodic then your problem is not too severe. Lay out your timings to conform to your picture cuts and try to match the picture cuts with musical values that pertain. Most film composers will lay out either a single line sketch, or a very simple sketch for overall timing. If they are orchestrating their own music, they will often work from this simplified sketch. If someone else is doing the orchestration, then they will complete the sketch for the orchestrator.

If the process of laying out timings involves rhythmic music, you are better off going to a click. Trying to speed up or slow down rhythmic music to catch cues can be mighty rough. If click tracks are not available to you, then you should resort to a Written Click Track*. Try to find an even tempo-per-bar to write to. For example, if you arrive at a tempo of :02 1/2 second per bar, the down-beat of bar 2 would be :02 1/2; bar 3 would be :05; bar 4 — :07 1/2, and so on. If you can keep the tempo even for a number of bars, you have a written click track. As long as the tempo stays constant, you can catch cues on or off of the beat. If there is a drastic change of tempo at a point in the cue, try to keep your written click track going evenly to that point and then make your change of tempo. If the cue is a dead cue and must be hit exactly, you might find some kind of a safety valve in the way of a trill bar, a percussion roll, or any other expedient device that gives you leeway to catch your cue. No matter how flexible you become in the use of the mechanics, your imagination as to how to get them to work for you is still the primary objective. In many cases where there is no real rhythmic feel, the use of the written click track is standard procedure. If the music is not really catching cues, but is moving along in a leisurely pace, you can lay out large blocks of timings in even stopwatch tempos. Example #19 demonstrates this point. The tempo has been moving in a steady 3/4 at :02 1/2 per bar. The example picks up the cue at bar 17. This is at :40 seconds. Although this cue is laid out for picture cueing, it is a perfect example of written click track — with some pertinent adjustments. From bar 17 through bar 28 the tempo remains constant. The orches-

See glossary

tration, however, allows the conductor quite a bit of freedom for rubato phrasing. On the downbeat of bar 29, the tempo has slowed down slightly. Friedhofer has indicated the timing speed on the score and the tempo has moved to :03 seconds per bar. At bar 33, the tempo speeds up slightly to allow time for the diminuendo to the F.F.O. (Full Fade Out), the end of the picture. Besides being a good example of fine timing technique, it is the perfect example of the way that the music and the orchestration work hand in hand to provide the nuances in the slight changes of tempos. Notice in bar 29 that as the tempo slows slightly, a trumpet solo starts a blues phrase with a triplet feel. Up to this point in the cue there has been nothing faster than an eighth note. The triplet figuration allows the tempo to slow down without being felt. This triplet blues figure is echoed in bar 30 by a flute; bar 31 by an accordion; and then relaxes into eighth notes to allow control to be exercised in bar 32 to hit the dead cue at bar 33. The speed up, (a tempo primo), in bar 33 is accentuated by the rush upwards in the woodwinds to provide a peak from which an effective diminuendo can be made for the F.F.O.

Up until the very end of this cue, the tempo was in the manner of a written click track. The music involved and the way it was set in the orchestration provided the most fluid natural kind of background to a dialogue scene imaginable.

If we were to apply the same technique to the previously discussed problem of laying out a single line timing sketch, it could work like this. We assumed that there was a picture obligation at :10 seconds and :23 1/3rd seconds. Using :02 1/2 seconds a bar as a working tempo, you could lay out timings each bar or every other bar before actually writing any music. This tempo would automatically take you to your first obligation at :10 seconds. Example 20 demonstrates this method.

The downbeat of bar 1 is :00. The D.B. of bar 2 is :02 1/2, bar 3 is :05, bar 4 is :07 1/2, the downbeat of bar 5 is your first cue — :10 seconds.In the next phrase which was from :10 seconds to :23 1/3rd seconds, you will have five full bars of approximately 2/3rd of a second left over that will have to be absorbed. This can be done by making the fifth bar of your second phrase, (bar 9 of the cue) a 4/4 bar. This added beat will pick up the 2/3rds of a second you need to hit your second cue at :23 1/3rd second. Naturally, you must have the music in mind when you pick your tempo. If your musical idea was in 5/4, your whole timing structure would have to be different to accommodate the music. The only purpose of this example is to illustrate that timings can be laid out in advance of writing music as long as you have the music in mind. Please remember that when we speak of first phrase and second phrase in these examples, they refer to timing phrases. They have nothing to do with musical phrases unless you desire to make them episodic. In almost every case, the musical concept must be an overall one from the start of the cue to the finish.

Even though you may not have click track facilities at your disposal, there is no reason why you can't use your metronome and stopwatch and lay out breakdowns that can be done in the written click track method. If the music is properly written to work at the pre-designated tempo, you can catch cues on or off the beat with almost the same security as having a click track going for you.

EXAMPLE #19

Record Band #4 ①

("I SPY" #38, M-62)

Comp: Hugo Friedhofer

EXAMPLE #19 (Cont.)

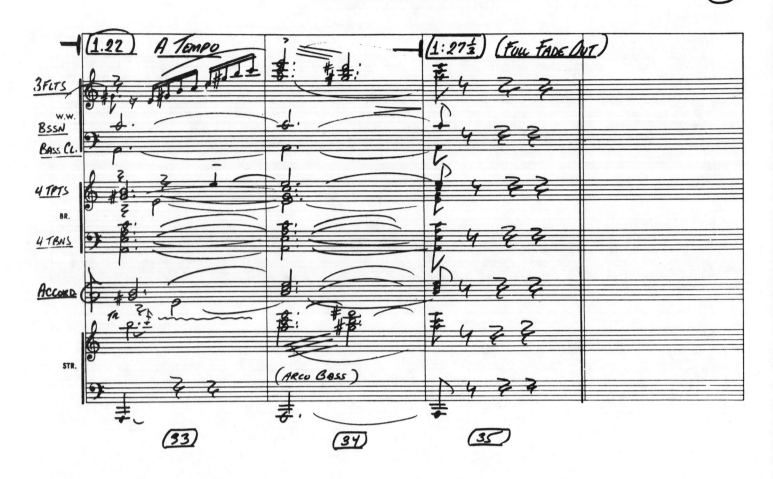

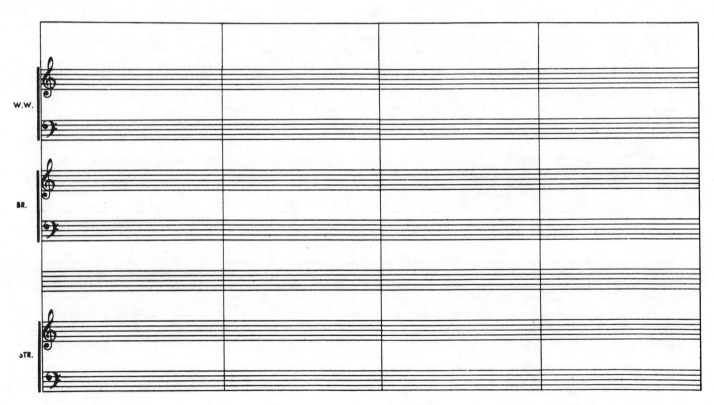

Prod. _____   Title ___EXAMPLE #20___   Page _____

Arranger _____

THE MECHANICS AND VOCABULARY
OF
FILM COMPOSITION

Always notate the stopwatch timing in the first bar of the score, and in any bars that involve a change of tempo. A metronome marking of 70 can mean many things to many people, but $3/4 = :02\ 1/2$ seconds can mean only one thing. At the rehearsal of the cue you can beat a bar or two to the watch to check your timing and rehearse your cue in the right tempo the first time. Any major variations in tempo such as: Rit., Rall., Poco Mosso, Poco Meno, Poco Tenuto, or such, should be marked on the score and copied in all of the orchestra parts. It is not necessary for the orchestra to have stopwatch timings; those are your problems, but you can cut down on a lot of conversation and confusion by having any subtle or drastic changes in tempo carefully marked for the musicians.

If there is any summation to be made on the value of careful timing, it would have to be in the area of keeping the music completely natural. Every cue you write should be checked and rechecked from the top. The music should flow smoothly and maintain a feeling of continuity from start to finish. At all times, it should sound like a complete piece of music. This is often the hardest achievement in film music writing. You are constantly at the mercy of the cuts and changes in the film. There will be times when you would give anything for another two seconds to make a phrase more natural. The tone poems you write are governed in feet of film and there will also be times when you will swear that the picture has been deliberately edited in a way to make your job impossible. The job is never impossible. There are many situations that you will run into that offer you all kinds of leeway. These are not nearly the test of your film technique as the ones that seem to be impossible. When you get the stopwatch in your hand and start to work on a cue, put this precept firmly in your mind, "if it doesn't time right when you write, it will never time right on the stage."

When I advise you to hear the orchestra accurately, you must take into consideration the characteristics of the individual instruments. For example: if you wrote a legato solo for clarinet in approximately :04 seconds a bar and decided to change it to a high cello solo, you had better allow :05 seconds a bar for the cello. The dramatic intensity of the cello needs time to register. Give it time. If you are using patterns with movement in them under a solo voice, take care to hear what kind of impact they will have on the overall effect; time them carefully. The ideal cue is one that sounds exactly on the stage as you heard it at home when you wrote it.

THE MECHANICS AND VOCABULARY
OF
FILM COMPOSITION

CHAPTER 10

PICTURE CUEING

Example #21 shows a cue marked for picture recording. There are many advantages to picture recording. First of all it eliminates the stopwatch. Secondly, it allows you to play back immediately with picture and dialogue and check to see and hear how the music fits. If there is any problem whatsoever, it will show up on the play back. You can make adjustments on the stage and record the cue again, knowing that the end result will fit perfectly. Picture recording should eliminate any music cutting after recording. The end result is always better, more homogeneous, and tailored perfectly to the picture. While the cost of picture recording is slightly higher, involving preparation on the part of the cutter, a dummy operator, and a projectionist, the end result reflects many savings in many areas. There is no post cutting to speak of, saving time and personnel. The end result fits better and saves time in dubbing. The product is always better because you have the opportunity to hear the product with picture and make necessary changes right then and there.

I SPY #11

M-26 PICTURE   St Mk 659

00   ✗3

K. enters hotel room in euphovia - S. tells
him - "Johnny's dead" - strangled right here-
look at the photos - Turn them over" - Start
as K. turns photo and we see : "Photo by Tatia
Loring"

.00-2/3   Cut. C.S. - K. looking stunned.

.01-1/3   S (O.S.) "Try for two." (ends .02)

.02-1/2   Cut. M.S. - K & S.

.04⅓   .04-2/3   He turns 2nd photo over and looks at it.

.06   S: "Now hit a home run." (ends .06-2/3)

.10-1/3   CUT - Insert

.10-2/3   K's hand picks up 3rd photo -

.11-1/3   - and flops it over - "Tatia Loring" again.

.11-2/3   Camera starts to zoom in -

.13   - Holds in E.C.S. of printing.

⊕ .17   .13-1/3   Cut - MCS - K. - trying to digest this.

.21-1/2   K.(quietly): "You're out of your mind."

.22-2/3   CUT - C.S. -S.

.23-2/3   S: "You flip over some chick that you didn't
⊕ .26½   know the day before yesterday, and when I tell
you she's involved in the death of those men-"

.30-1/2   CUT - C.S. -K. - S.(cont, O.S.): - You tell
⊕ .31½   me I'm out of my mind."

.33   CUT - C.S. - S.

.33-13   S(cont): " - O.K. -- you better straighten up,
Jack."

.37-2/3   CUT - C.S. - K.

.38-1/3   K: "Just because she's got a photo credit on
three pictures??"

(Continued)

EXAMPLE #21   Record Band #5

"TRY FOR TWO"

"I SPY" #11   M-26   EARLE HAGEN

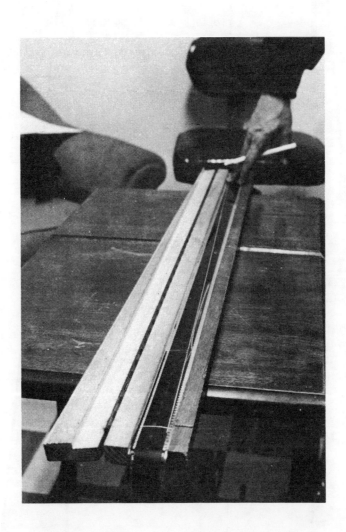

EXAMPLE #22   The Streamer Board

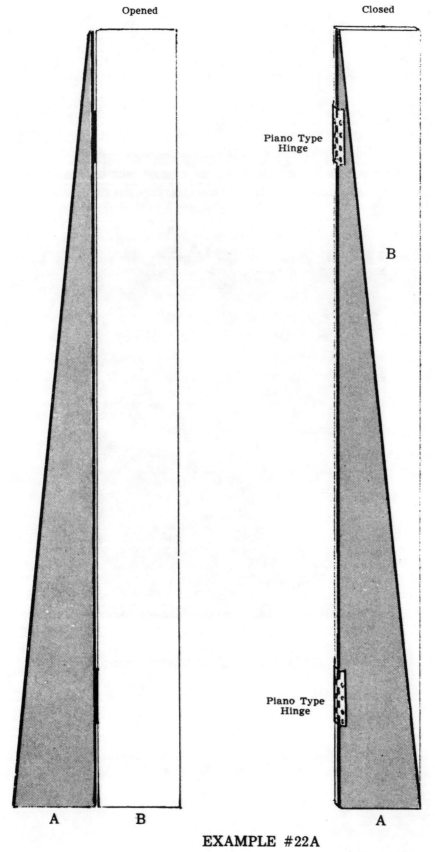

Opened

Closed

Piano Type
Hinge

B

A   B

Piano Type
Hinge

A

EXAMPLE #22A

Homemade 3′ Streamer Board Made Out Of 2 Yard Sticks

There are two kinds of basic picture recording: picture cueing, and dialogue cueing.

In the first case, the picture, (usually a Work Print*), Streamers*, which are lines that move across the screen, and Punches*, which are bursts of light, are generally used. In the second instance, a streamer usually starts the cue; the conductor listens to the dialogue track and usually takes his cueing from the dialogue. In dialogue recording as well as picture cueing, the stopwatch writing technique remains the same. The dialogue cues, usually the end of sentences or exclamations, are timed on the cue sheet to the 3rd or 2/3rds of a second. A slight allowance has to be made to clear the ends of the words. In T.V. music, especially comedy shows, dialogue recording is not too practical. Most comedy shows use a laugh track and the laughs generally fall exactly where the musical reaction would start. Picture cueing with streamer technique can be made tighter and more accurate. Another disadvantage, to my way of thinking, is that dialogue recording commits the conductor to listen to the dialogue rather than the orchestra. Very few conductors use the dialogue method. It is slower recording method, as a dummy operator must thread up the dialogue track for the take and then rewind and thread up again for the playback. The use of this method is strictly a matter of personal taste. Those composers who are familiar with it prefer it to any other.

The more commonly used method of the two is picture cueing. The two devices that form the basis of picture cueing are the Streamer* and the Punch*. The streamer is used to start the cue, to catch dead cues and to end cues. A streamer is a line that travels across the screen from left to right. When it hits the right edge of the screen, you are on your cue. The major studios have machines that scribe streamer lines in different lengths. The length of the streamer is a matter of individual taste and comfort. Streamers are usually 3, 4, 5 or six feet in length, being 2, 2-2/3rds, 3-1/3rd, and 4 seconds in travel left to right. The 3 foot streamer is the most commonly used one in the T.V. industry because you don't need a complex machine to make one.

A simple streamer board can be made out of two yard sticks. Taper one from the top edge of one side to the bottom edge of the other side. Hinge the two together so that the top board when folded over is tapered from left to right. Two brads at the top and bottom can be used to hold the film in place. Mark the frame of your dead cue; place the film on the streamer board with the start of the dead cue at the bottom. Slip the sprocket holes over the brads and turn over the tapered board on top of the film. Scribe a line on the film with a 3/16th inch carpenters nail set. You now have a streamer to your dead cue. The visual effect of a streamer is a line panning across the screen from left to right. Some composers like a punch at the end of the streamer to mark the dead cue. With a three foot streamer, the time of travel is 2 seconds. This doesn't sound like much, but is sufficient when the music is timed right.

The punch is a burst of light and is used as a guide post to mark relative timings on the way to the streamer. To make a punch, the frame corresponding to the timing indicated is marked. A hand punch, similar to the kind used to punch notebook paper, is used to punch out the cue. Another punch is added two frames on either side of the critical timing. This gives you three punches spread over five frames. The effect of the punch is a flash of light that you can see without taking your eyes off of the score. The length of the punches used are once again a matter of personal taste. Some composers prefer longer punches. The limit is usually 10 punches over a 20 frame spread. The reason for the skipped frame between punches is to keep the film from tearing as it passes through the projector.

The way streamers and punches are used is as follows:

Example #21A is a score that is marked for streamers and punches.

The streamer marking looks like this: ——|

The punch mark looks like this: +

You will notice that the punch marks are placed on top of the desired timings and the streamers are marked to the exact timing and the exact beat where they are needed. Most timings are notated at the top of the score where they can be seen with a glance. To put them inside of the score is usually confusing. They are almost always marked with a heavy marking pen or a colored marking pen or pencil. They must always be easily located.

In Example #21 you will see that the first streamer is lined up to :00. This means that the streamer has been marked in the last three feet of the twenty foot leader. A twenty foot leader is also added to the dialogue track so that the picture and dialogue can be played back in synch. In the music of Example #21, the orchestra starts with the streamer at :00. The music is conducted rubato to the downbeat of bar 3, the next streamer. The next two bars are also rubato. The streamer is used again at :11 1/3 sec. for the next Dead Cue.* From this point on, we have no dead cues to hit so we go to the punch technique. The tempo of bar 8 has been very carefully notated on the score as :05 sec. per bar. There is a punch at :26 1/2 sec. If you are moving too fast or ahead at the downbeat at bar 9 (:26 1/2 sec.), you will hit this downbeat before you see the flash of the punch. You slow down the tempo slightly and try to land on the downbeat of bar 10 with the punch at :31 1/3 sec. If you are on the punch at the downbeat of bar 10 (:31 1/3 sec.), the :02 sec. spread that a three foot streamer takes to cross the screen will guarantee the next dead cue :37 2/3 sec. at the downbeat of bar 11. Generally, it is not a good idea to go more than :10 sec. without a punch. You could drift far enough off to make it impossible to catch your streamer. It is also a good idea to have a punch on the downbeat of the bar before a streamer, providing the tempo is not too fast. This gives you a chance to make a final tempo adjustment to catch your streamer. Remember, the punches do not really count. They are only a means to keep you in relative timing so you can hit the streamer. The streamer is the only thing that is imperative.

In the case of necessary changes in bar times to catch your streamers, there are all kinds of adjustments that you can make. Example #23A starts in a :04 sec. per bar tempo until bar 4. The streamer at :12 1/3rd is picked up by a slight broadening of the last two beats of the phrase in the celli. The tempo then holds to :04 sec. per bar to pick up the streamer at :20 1/3rd sec. The tempo still holds at :04 sec. per bar and picks up the punch at :28 1/3rd sec. The :04 sec. per bar tempo holds through to the downbeat of bar 10 where a punch :36 1/3rd sets you up for a critical cue. The next streamer is at :41 2/3rds. This is a lapse of :05 sec. You have been moving at 1 sec. per beat, so the natural thing to do is to add a beat and make bar 10 a 5/4 bar. This picks up the streamer at :41 2/3rds. Notice that the movement in bar 10 tapers off to give a rubato effect. Bar 11 through 15 hold to the original tempo of :04 sec. per bar and pick up the streamer at :57 2/3rds. The streamers at 1:00 1/2 and 1:02 1/2 are completely unrelated as far as tempo is concerned and involve powerful picture effects. There is very little movement in bar 15 or 16. The time values of these bars were designed to make the build up to the scream at 1:00 1/2 sec. The impact at 1:02 1/2 was allowed to ring until it died away. This gave the effect of the drama of the scream hanging over the next scene, until dialogue.

Study this cue sheet carefully. The story point is self-evident — then, take a stopwatch and conduct through this cue. You should be able to feel the amount of freedom that you have even though you are meeting timings.

See glossary

EXAMPLE #23

I SPY #43   411'

St,mk 391

M-41
(T 1)

Kelly has just visited Tonia and corrected his impression of her - he finds her to be sincere in her feelings about Scott. He is just taking leave from her apartment and says: " GOOD LUCK. " She says: " THANK YOU. "

:00   Music Starts just as Kelly starts toward door.

:08   He stops on the threshold.

:10 1/3   He asks: " IT'S O.K. IF I CLOSE THE DOOR NOW? " (Ends :12 1/3)

:12 1/3   Cut to M.S. Tonia - smiling.

:12 2/3   Tonia answers: " YES, 'CIAO'. " (Ends L14)

:14 2/3   Cut back to Kelly.

:15 1/3   He repeats: " 'CIAO'." (Ends :15 2/3)

:20 1/3   Cut to Tonia - happy now.

:21   She gives big sigh of relief.

:25 2/3   Picks up bouquet and starts toward kitchen.
:28/3
:29 1/2   Cut to Kelly M.S. in hall just outside Tonia's apartment. He is tearing up the false note that brought him to see Tonia.

:36 1/3
:37 1/3   He lets pieces fall on small table O.S. outside her door, as camera starts pan to table.

:38 1/3   Camera stops pan on torn pieces as Kelly leaves.

:39 2/3   Cut to Tonia busy in kitchen.

:41 2/3   She makes a slight reaction as though she might have heard something.

:42 1/2   She listens a little more carefully.

:46 1/3   She asks: " IS THAT YOU KELLY - DID YOU FORGET SOMETHING? " (Ends :48 1/3)
:49 2/3
:53 1/2   She starts slowly toward door.

:55 2/3   Cut to open doorway - no one in sight.

:57 2/3   Tonia looks to one side out of doorway.

                                          (cont'd.)

EXAMPLE #23 (Cont.)

I SPY #43

M-41 (P. 2.)

:59 1/3   She turns to look into camera.

:59 2/3   Her expression starts into terror.

1:00 1/2   She starts blood-curdling scream as camera
               moves in closer.

1:02 1/2   Cut to C.U. sign: "Officers' Club-U.S. Armed Forces"

1:04 2/3   Start Dissolve

1:06 2/3   Full In on Full Shot of Kelly standing in lush
               lounge room of Officers' Club-no one else present.

Hold Long   TOTAL TIME 1:06 2/3

Prod. _____   Title ____ EXAMPLE #23 A (Cont.) ____   Page ___②___

Arranger _____

Example #24A is a picture cue that involves more tempo latitudes than the previous one. Study the cue sheet first to absorb the scene. Although seeing the picture would naturally be much better than just looking at a cue sheet, the cue sheet is well enough detailed for you to get the meaning of the scene and the problems imposed upon the composer. :00 starts in 8/8 with a ferocious passage in violins. The 8/8 time value was to be able to subdivide the string passage to hold it together. The streamer at :07 2/3rds was a natural timing for the pace of the string passage. Bars three and four tapered off in intensity and at :15 sec. the cue relaxed completely, setting up the English horn solo. From the streamer at :20 seconds, the tempo resolved into :05 sec. per bar and held through bar 13. From bar 14 on the tempo picked up to :03 1/2 sec. per bar and the intensity of the background accompaniment increased in dissonance to match the scene. There is an inside subtlety at the streamer at 1:19 1/3rd. This was accomplished by simply adding a shade more weight in the background. The basic new tempo of :03 1/2 sec. per bar holds until bar 23 where a Rall. is indicated to catch the smoke at 1:36 2/3rds. Conduct through this cue with the stopwatch.

All of these examples have been recorded for specific films and all of them work exactly in they way they are supposed to. Note that at the end of this cue there was no timing. The last effect was held long and dialed out under the ensuing dialogue.

To make your timings natural, move the bar line, affect rubatos, take any musical license you please, but be sure that you have timed it correctly.

We have discussed the written click track. It is much easier to do with picture. If you have a tempo in mind, you can punch every bar and give yourself a visual click track. The orchestra will not see it, but it can most certainly keep the conductor in the right tempo. There will be times when you will have violent changes of tempo and do not hesitate to punch every bar of the new tempo if necessary. Any usage of the mechanics that will enable you to get a better end result is valid.

Another adjustment that you can make to drop a beat is to have your streamer at :00 be part of a pick up bar. There is no rule that says that a cue must start on a downbeat. It can start anywhere. If you have to add or lose beats anywhere in a cue, look for a place that is natural. It can occur just before the streamer or at the beginning, or anywhere else in the music.

Remember, when you lay out your cue sheet, circle the important timings. These will probably wind up as streamers. The punches can be added as you construct your music. Always aim your punches towards the streamers.

Quite often there will be cues that start with a demand for clicks and then go to free timing. This is the subject of the next chapter.

EXAMPLE #24   103

I SPY #43   400'

M-24

A big brawl has started in the Cantina
where Scott was trying to make a pitch
to Tonia about America. In the melee Tonia
get konked C.U. to camera-right on the knob.

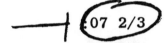 :00   Music Starts as Tonia is konked with bottle.

:00 2/3   Cut to a big guy coming in to sock somebody.

:01 1/2   He gets smashed on jaw.

:02   Cut to Close on Scott bending over to pick up
          Tonia as brawl continues.

:05 1/3   He raises her up on his shoulder and starts
          to carry her out away from danger.

:07 2/3   Start Dissolve.

:09 2/3   Full In on C.U. Scott's hands at wash basin
          wetting a padded towel.

:10 1/3   Camera starts panning L. It passes C.U. to
          kitchen range, etc.

:13 2/3   Camera stops pan-centered on open doorway showing
          Tonia lying on bed in neat room.

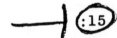 :15   Cut to M.C.U. Tonia on bed.

:18 2/3   Scott's hands seen gently applying wet towel to
          her head injury.

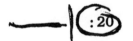 :20   Her eyes indicate she's beginning to come back
          to consciousness.

:22 1/2   She casts an anxious look across room as if to
          ask 'Where am I?' and camera starts pulling back.

:24 2/3   She starts to rise up but Scott restrains her gently
          as he says " NN,NN, I WOULDN'T DO THAT JUST YET. "
          (Ends :27 1/2 as camera stops pull back)

:27 2/3   She asks: " HOW DID YOU FIND MY ROOM? "

:30   Scott answers as he moistens a pad with alcohol:
          " THERE'S A LITTLE OLD MAN LIVES IN A ROOM BACK
          OF THE BAR TOLD ME WHERE YOU LIVED. CUTE LITTLE
          GUY WITH EYE-GLASSES. " (Ends :35 1/3)

:36 2/3   As he leans over to apply the alcohol to her head,
          he says: " NOW THIS IS GOING TO STING-JUST A
          LITTLE. " (Ends :39 1/2)

:39   He places pad on her wound.
:40
:40 1/3   Cut to C.U. Tonia-Scott's hand holds pad to her
          head.

(Cont'd.)

EXAMPLE #24 (Cont.)

I SPY #43

M-24 (P. 2.)

:42 1/3   Cut to C.U. Scott.

:42 2/3   Scott observes: " YOU HOLD YOUR ALCOHOL PRETTY
             WELL, YOU DIDN'T EVEN FLINCH. " (Ends :45)

:45 1/2   Cut to C.U. Tonia.

:46   Tonia - a little defensively: " I DO NOT FEEL
             PAIN. " (Ends :47 1/2)

:47 2/3   Cut to C.U. Scott.

:48 1/3   Scott: " WELL THAT'S A FUNNY WAY TO LIVE YA KNOW,
             HOW YA GONNA KNOW WHEN YOU'RE HURT?" (Ends :51)

:51   Cut to C.U. Tonia.

:51 2/3   Tonia-still a bit defensive-answers: " THERE'S
             NOTHING WRONG WITH THE WAY I LIVE-I'M INDEPENDENT,
             AND I HAVE MY OWN BUSINESS. " (Ends :56)

:56   Cut to C.U. Scott.

:57   Scott adds sardonically: " CREEPING CAPITALISM. "
             (Ends :58 2/3)

:58 2/3   Cut to M.S. Scott moving from bedside as camera
             follows him.

:59 2/3   O.S. Tonia says: " EVEN IN SOCIALIST COUNTRIES
             THERE IS PRIVATE ENTERPRISE. " (Ends 1:04 2/3)

1:04 2/3   Cut to C.U. Scott.

1:05 1/3   Scott-wryly: " WELL, IT WAS JUST MY OWN LITTLE
             PERSONAL JOKE-YA KNOW. THANK YOU FOR LAUGHING. "
             (Ends 1:10)

1:10 1/3   Cut to C.U. Tonia-still lying back on pillow.

1:12 1/3   She says-business like: " I THANK YOU FOR YOUR
             HELP, MR. SCOTT. AND NOW, I HAVE WORK TO DO- I
             MUST BAKE MY PIES FOR TOMORROW. (Ends 1:19 1/3)

1:19 1/3   Cut to Full Shot Tonia getting up and away from bed.

1:21 1/3   Tonia stops and places hand on head-in pain.

1:22 1/3   Cut to Full Shot Scott in neat room-camera pans
             L as he starts to rush to her side.

1:24 1/2   He grabs her around waist as she totters a little.

1:25   She protests as he starts to put her back to bed:
             " NO, NO, NO, I HAVE PIES FOR TOMORROW-THERE'LL
             BE NOTHING TO SELL---."

                                            (cont'd.)

EXAMPLE #24 (Cont.)

I SPY #43

M-24 (P. 3.)

1:28

1:29   Scott breaks in: " SURE YOU DO, " as he
        places her back on pillow.

1:30 1/3   He continues: " NOW, LISTEN, WE'RE GOING TO HAVE
            TO MAKE AN INSTRUMENT LANDING, O.K.?"

1:35   As he rises to go to kitchen, he continues: "AND
        I BAKE PIES - THE CRUSTIEST." (Ends 1:36 1/2)

1:36 2/3   Start Dissolve.

1:38 2/3   Full In on C.U. of old fashioned cook-stove with
            oven-smoke coming from sides of the oven door.

1:39 2/3   Scott's hand grabs oven door-handle.

1:40 2/3   Music Ends as Oven door is dropped open and
            reveals a haze cloud of smoke.

                                    Total Time 1:40 2/3

Prod. _____   Title **EXAMPLE #24 A** (Cont.)   Composer _____
Arranger _____

Prod. _____   Title   EXAMPLE #24 A (Cont.)   Composer _____
Arranger _____

EXERCISES AND SELF-ANALYSIS

There are no exercises that can be developed for free timing cues inasmuch as they involve conducting rather than math. The problem is to make the music flow both from the conductor's standpoint and the orchestra's. Naturally, writing cues to stopwatch is necessary, but only if you can prove it out with an orchestra. All of the cues in this book have been written for specific films, recorded, and proven. In lieu of any other means of exercise, I would suggest that you conduct these cues to stopwatch and get the feel of the way they flow from cue to cue.

This should not discourage you in any way from writing cues for orchestra, but the real test is how they will time when actually put to work.

There are a lot of examples in this book that are written for free timing. Even though they may be for some other purpose, take the time to conduct through them with a stopwatch. All of the examples have been proven on the recording stage. I think that as you conduct them over and over again to stopwatch, you'll begin to get the feeling of how flexible free timing really is.

CHAPTER 11
CLICK TRACKS TO FREE TIMING

Many situations arise where there is a picture obligation that involves a combination of click track and free timing procedure; the front part of the the cue calling for rigid tempo, and the back part of the cue allowing for the freedom of free timing. Example #25 is such a case. The tempo in the beginning was fast and exciting; then at :26 2/3rds the necessity for excitement passed and the obligation became one of soft menace under _soft_ dialogue. The click track was laid out to carry the cue to :26 2/3rds and then the clicks were stopped and the cue went on in free timing. The cutter builds his click track in the tempo designated, in this case 10 frames, and then goes to marking the picture with streamers and punches. Picture cueing of any kind always demands the use of a Work Print*. A cheap copy of the original negative is run off as a work print or dupe (duplicate.) All of the editing crafts mark this positive film, scribe it, often tear and repair it, and generally give it a real beating. No matter what they do to it, it has no effect on the original negative, which is not cut until the picture is completely finished and dubbed. Obviously, if you are working on a film that has not or is not going to be duped, you must forget picure cueing of the scribe and punch technique. Streamers can be put on an original film with black tape. It is not ideal, but it does work.

*See glossary

EXAMPLE #25

<u>I SPY #38</u>   755'

M-14/21   **PICTURE**

:00   K's **two** friends from back home have brought him
           a watch. Jana, **who happens** to be their tour guide,
           looks at the watch and drops it, breaking the
           crystal. She tells them not to worry, that she
           knows a place where she can get it fixed in an
           emergency and that she can get it back to their
           hotel that evening by six o'clock. She leaves
           them as they say good-bye. The Doctors says -
           "THAT'S ONE NICE GIRL." START <u>On Cut</u> after this
           to Jana coming down stairway.

:05 1/3   She, still running, rounds a corner in front of
           a yellow phone booth.

:08 2/3   She has circled around the booth and **heads** up
           another flight of steps.

:14 1/3   Cut to a **shot** of **a** bridge, coming from a darkened
           archway.

:14 2/3   Jana is seen entering bridge, still running.

:17 2/3   She disappears to building on other side.

:18 1/3   Cut to Int. Shot of doorway of Heavy's room.

:20   Jana enters.

:23 1/2   She walks around corner.

:27   She **places** article in front of Heavy, who is
           sitting at desk **examining** goods.

:28 2/3   He looks up as she says - "IT NEEDS A NEW
           MECHANISM."

:31 2/3   Heavy - "HUH. WHEN?"

:35 2/3   Jana - "BY SIX O'CLOCK TONIGHT."

:38   Heavy - "WE'LL HAVE MORE THAN ENOUGH TIME." He is
           examining the watch.
                                          window,
:41 1/3   She turns and walks toward/exit twirling her glove.

:46   Jana (seating herself in chair in front of window)-
           "WHY DO YOU TAKE THIS ROUND-ABOUT WAY...HUH?"

                                              (cont'd)

EXAMPLE #25A (Cont.)

EXAMPLE #25 A (Cont.)

If you examine the cue sheet of this example, you will see the action indicated and where the cutter has been instructed to stop the clicks and go to free timing. This was a very long cue and there was no reason to print all of it, once the technical point was made. This again was a self constructed bar breakdown, as you can tell by the numbered clicks. When laying out a breakdown, don't hesitate to number every click. It is easy to make a mistake in click numbers, especially if you are shifting around your time values. Any mistakes in click numbers will throw your music far off in the actual recording. Another example of the use of clicks to free timing is shown in Example #26. Only the last 6 bars of this cue have been used for the example. The previous 40 bars of music were going along in a 14-4 click track and at the 171st click (1:42 2/3rds.) a piece of action occurs that allows the click to be broken and free timing to take over to catch the direct overlap at 1:48 1/3rd. This could have been clicked out to the end of the cue, but the action called for a big effect in the orchestra and seemed better in the free timing mode. This is again a matter of personal taste. The more of the mechanical background you have at your command, the more ways you will find to handle situations of this kind. The right solution is the one that is right for you and allows you to express yourself in the method that appeals to your own taste. You will notice on the cue sheets that involve endings to commercials, or ending to the picture (F.F.O.)* there is a notation of "1/2 second allowed". This means that the last timing ends 1/2 second before the full fade out of the picture and allows for the natural or artificial reverberation of the orchestra cut off to die away. Room tone or reverb-natural or artificial-take up time, and this time must be allowed for or the track will sound chopped-off.

Obviously, clicks to free timing can be used with stopwatch if you are not using picture cueing. You stop your clicks at the designated point and continue the cue with the stopwatch. Be sure that you start your watch at :00 of the cue.

There may be cases where you wish to start a cue in free timing and then go to clicks. The most practical way of doing this is to come to a hold just before your clicks start and have a couple of warning clicks as pickups to establish the incoming tempo. If your music allows for the slight stall, you are all right. If it doesn't, this can be an awkward situation and may be better handled by the use of overlaps or segues. These will be discussed in detail later in this book.

See glossary

116

EXAMPLE #26

I SPY #38

M-11 (P. 2)

12'	:55 2⍉3	Cut to MS Jana sitting on a launch as it moves along.
	:57 2/3	Cut to Reverse Angle - Her POV.
	1:02 1/3	Cut to man on bridge above, looking down.
newtopM11A	1:04 2/3 [00]	Cut back to Jana sitting on boat.
14-4 cl	1:06 1/2	She, looking around very concerned, says - SOMETHING IN ITALIAN to the man running the boat.
	1:08 1/3 :03⅔	Cut back to her POV.
	1:09 1/3 :04⅔	He looks back at her, nodding slightly.
clk (12)	1:11 1/3 :06½	Cut back to man on bridge.
	1:12 1/2	He turns away from railing as if to leave.
	1:13 1/3	Cut to launch from bridge POV as it moves up to landing.
	1:17 2/3 :13	The driver of the boat leaves the wheel and walks over to help Jana out of launch.
	1:23 1/2 32 18¾	Cut back to man on bridge. He appears oblivious to the whole scene.
	1:25 2/3 :21	Cut to launch as it speeds off. Camera is doing fast pan over to Jana, who is walking up the steps.
	1:28 2/3 :24	She looks up toward the man.
	1:29 :24⅓	Cut back to man on bridge.
	1:29 2/3	He looks down at her.
clk 45+	1:31 2/3 .27	Cut back to his POV of Jana looking up.
	1:32 2/3 .29	She holds her right hand up to her forehead as though shading her eyes, and places her left hand, palm up, on her left shoulder.
	1:34 1/3 .30⅔	Still in this position, she nods slightly.
	1:34 1/2 :30¾	Cut to man on bridge.

(cont'd)

EXAMPLE #26 (Cont.)

I SPY #38

M-11A (P. 3)

1:35 1/3	:30 2/3	He, pretending indifference, raises two fingers.
1:36 1/2	:31 3/4	He begins to move off the bridge.
1:37 1/3	:32 2/3	Cut to LS of him over Jana's shoulder as he moves off bridge. Her eyes follow him until he is obscured by a large pillar.
1:42 1/3	:37 2/3	She turns back toward Camera with a complacent expression, and moves out of frame.
1:47		Cut to the man as he enters frame looking for her.
1:48 1/3	.43 2/3	He spots her and moves over to her.
⑦⑥ 1:50	(.45 1/3)	The man says - "A BRUNETTE .. THEY SAID YOU WOULD BE BLONDE."
1:53 2/3	.49	Jana - "BUT I WAS TIRED OF BEING A BLONDE .. SO .. THIS MORNING I BECAME A BRUNETTE. DO YOU MIND?"
1:59 1/2		Cut to MCU of him over her shoulder. He says - "IN OUR PROFESSION, LUCK AND CAUTION ARE THE SAME THING."
⑨⑧ 2:03	58 2/3	Cut back to Reverse Angle.
2:03 2/3	59 1/3	She acknowledges this with a nod.
101 2:04 1/2	1:00 3/4	Jana says - SOMETHING INDISTINGUISHABLE.
108 2:08 1/2	1:04 2/4	He steps down to face her as she begins to remove a pendant from around her neck.
2:12 1/3	1:07 2/3	She gives it to him.
2:15 1/3	1:10 2/3	He reaches into his coat for a small key.
2:16 2/3	1:12	Cut to CU - His hand holding the pendant.
2:17 1/3	1:12 2/3	He inserts key into bottom of pendant.
125+ 2:20	1:15 1/3	As he turns key in pendant, he says - "GOOD ENOUGH."
2:21	1:16 1/3	Cut to CU of him as he continues - "....BUT NEXT TIME, I MUST BE INFORMED OF ANY CHANGE IN HAIR COLOR."

(cont'd)

EXAMPLE #26 (Cont.)

<u>I SPY #38</u>

M-114 (P. 4)

138 2:27 1/2 1.22¾ Cut to CU Jana.

139 2:28 — 1:23⅝ Jana - "I'M SORRY. THERE WASN'T TIME TO INFORM ANYBODY."

145 2:31 2/3 127 Cut to CU of her hand.

2:32 1/3 - 127⅔ Jana ⊤(as she begins pulling something from her handbag) - "HOLIDAY IN VENICE, JANOS .. TIME TO RELAX." (Ends 2:36)

151 2:35 1/3 130⅔ She has a knife in her hand.

2:36 1/2 Cut to CU The two of them. xxxJana-(as he leans toward her, amorously) - "WHY DON'T YOU BEGIN .. BY RETURNING MY TOKEN .. HUH?" (2:43)-(Ends)

2:43 1/2 He prepares to put the pendant back over head.

165 2:43 2/3 — 139 Cut to CU Lower half of Jana.

2:44 1/2 Her hand drops down with knife poised in it.

167 2:45 — 1:40⅝ The blade flashes out.

2:46 2/3 142 Her hand moves out of frame with knife poised.

171 2:47 2/3 1:43⁴²·⁷ He cries out in pain as she sticks it in him.

2:48 1/3 His body buckles in to hers.

2:48 2/3 Cut to CU His face,/xxx leaning over him like a Black Widow. Jana

2:49 They slowly sink out of frame.

2:50 2/3 1.46 Cut to ground as he falls.

177⁺ 2:51 1/2 1.46⅞ He hits ground.

2:53 — 1.48⅝ Cut to Main Title.

TOTAL TIME 2:53

EXAMPLE #26A

THE MECHANICS AND VOCABULARY
OF
FILM COMPOSITION

Example #27 shows an extreme problem which required an extreme solution. Of necessity, a pre-recorded vocal was photographed to a guide track and the problem was to set up the musical concept that the number had been going on for some time; provide a vocal background to the number, and make a finish that would sound like an ending to a Las Vegas production. The problems of guide tracks and pre-recorded vocals will be examined later in context, but the mechanics used apply to this part of the book. The cue sheet for this cue doesn't begin to show the problems involved. A great deal of time at the Moviola was necessary to set this cue up and arrive at the best possible way of attacking it.

You will notice on the score that clix were used at the beginning to bring us into the vocal. Streamers were used to set each line of the vocal, which was sung rubato, and then clicks were used again in a faster tempo to lock the orchestra to the action of the dance and vocal to the finish.

This is an extreme situation and reflects the possibilities offered by the use of the mechanics. The show character had to be firmly in mind to select the tempo of the starting click. The useage of streamers to catch the rubato vocal was the only practical way to accomplish a locked in vocal background. The orchestration was kept simple to allow the conductor the greatest amount of freedoom. The use of the pick up clicks to set the final tempo was practical because there was a slight stall before the final section of the vocal and the pick up clicks were set into what was aurally a natural hold. The click tempo for the ending section locked the vocal and orchestra together for voice and action synch and the whole layout gave this short, but difficult, vocal problem the feeling of continuity that made the final product sound as though the voice, dancers, and visual action had been performed live in a Las Vegas nightclub.

This is a perfect example of the mechanics applied.

Let's examine this same problem with the handicap of no picture facilities whatsoever. If you had clicks available, you could use them to get you into the cue. If not, you would have to stay with the stopwatch and get to a chord at :03.4 seconds that accommodates the pick up into the vocal. Then each bar could be made separately until bar 11. If each bar is made slightly overlong, the center can be cut out of the bar to fit the next chordal entrance. At bar 11 you could record a separate short phrase that takes you to the downbeat of bar 16. To keep the tempo, you should do this as a written click track with a timing on every bar. The last chord is made Wild*, or separately. For protection in this kind of bind, you should make every part of this sequence several different tempos. You will be depending on the background to be cut to fit and if you are a little on the long side of your cues, you are safe. Without picture or click facilities, you would have to make this cue in several separate pieces. The end result would not be nearly as smooth, but under the circumstances it would be the best you could hope for. It may not be the perfect way to go about it, but it can be done. What you have done in effect is a grouping of segues. Segues and overlaps are a large part of the musical mechanical technique and should be examined in detail.

*See glossary

EXAMPLE #27

8.0 dx
12 FREE

T 1

CHICK #1

M 13 REVISED - SWEETNER FOR VOCAL 77 ft.

END CLX
11th CLY
12th CLY

:00   F.I. from comm'l - F.S. marquee reading
           "Jerry Wallace-Vive La Difference Revue."

:03 2/3   On start of diss. to int., we hear Jerry
           singing "WHEN I'M NOT NEAR---"

"I'M"   :07   "---THE GIRL---"

"NEAR"

+ 2nd Note
"NEAR"   :08 2/3   "---I LOVE---" (Ends :10 2/3)

           :10 1/2
           :11 1/3   He pulls girl to him.

1 CLK WARN
12-4 CLY   :12   And bends over.

           :12 1/3   Cut C.S. Jerry leaning over.

           :12 1/2   Second girl leans in next to him.

           :13 1/2   Third girl leans over him as he looks up to
                      camera.

           :14 1/3   Jerry: "...I LOVE THE GIRL I'M NEAR." (Ends
                      :16)

           :16 1/3   Laugh. (Ends :17)

           :17 1/3   Cut M.S. Jerry & girls.

19th
CLY   :18   Last chord.

           :18 1/2   Applause starts.

           Check against record.

           TOTAL TIME - :18

           NOTE: M 14 STARTS AT :20 2/3.

Prod. _____ Title EXAMPLE #27A (Cont.) Composer _____
Arranger *Pg. 2.*

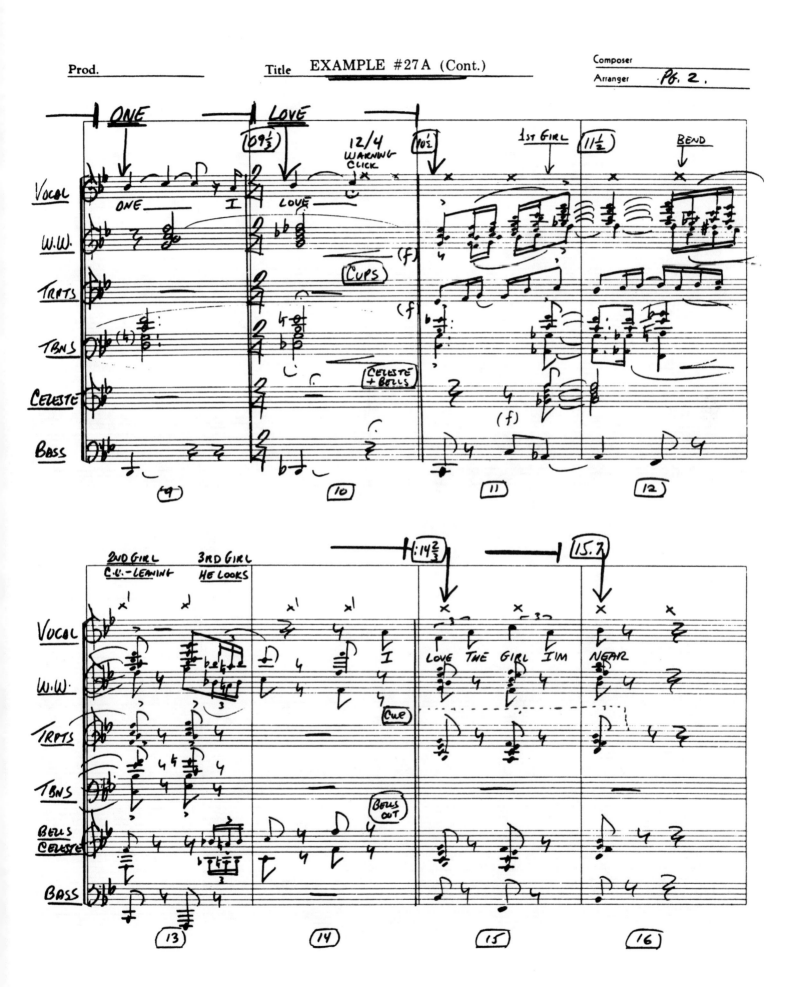

Prod. _____   Title   EXAMPLE #27A (Cont.)   Composer _____
                                                        Arranger PG. 3.

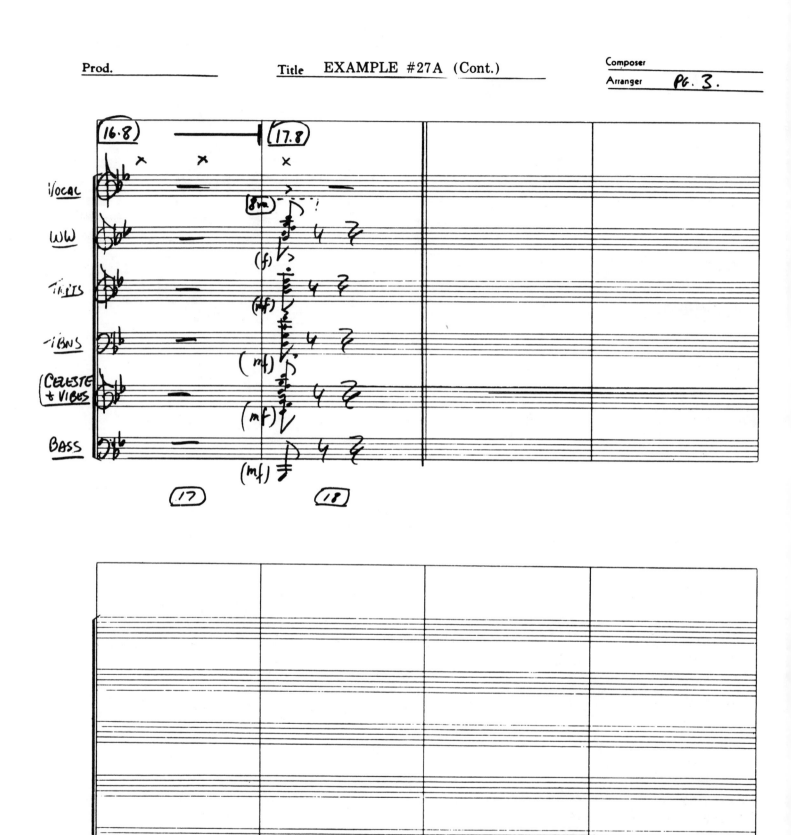

CHAPTER 12
SEGUES AND OVERLAPS

There really is no such musical designation as a segue in the film music business. There are many operations that serve as musical segues, but in the true sense of the word, they are regarded strictly as overlaps. Any music cue that come to a finish before starting again would be broken down as separate cue from the one that follows. Even if there were only a fraction of a second from the end of one cue to the beginning of another, in the film way of recording, these would be two separate cues and might be recorded at two different and widely separated times. Therefore, even though the end result sounds like a segue, it never really is. Any two cues that meet are categorized as Overlaps* or overlapping cues. There are many of these and their function in our overall accumulation of film technique is extremely important.

As it is the purpose of this book to not only clarify all of the possibilities, but categorize them as a reference manual, we will go into every aspect of the method and different kinds of overlaps.
#1. The overlap within a cue.

There are many situations that demand the splitting of a cue into two or more parts. The reason can be because the cue is extremely long and cutting it into two or more pieces gives the orchestra some rest, or allows the recording engineer to reset for sections that might offer difficult recording problems. While it is usual to duplicate the orchestration on both ends of the overlap, there are times when you want to reset the orchestration. The overlap gives you a chance to do this. Overlaps can be made from click track to click track; click track to free timing; free timing to click, and free timing to free timing. All of these will be examined before we go into the psychological types of overlaps.

Example 28—The overlap within a cue from click track to click track.

This cue, "I SPY" #56—M52/61, had been going on for 3:05 minutes. An opportunity to change tempo and the basic recording set-up presented itself at that timing. The tempo up to this time had been a 7-2 click track. The overlap was made at the down beat of bar 154. The chord on that down beat was held with a diminuendo. Bar 1 of M52/61-A, the second part of this cue, starts with exactly the same held chord which is orchestrated in the same way. The downbeat of bar 154, M52/61, is an exact duplicate of the downbeat of bar 1 of M52/61-A. However, the tempo goes from 4/4 in a 7-2 click track to 12/8 in a 14-4 click track. The re-recording problems of combining the two tracks will be discussed later. The A reel has the original track on it. The B reel has the second part and until the entrance of the second part, this reel is leadered out. When the two tracks are re-recorded, the overlap is unnoticeable.

See glossary

EXAMPLE #28

I SPY #56

MS2/61, A — 364
St. mk. — 344'

M-52 (P. 5)

	2:54 2/3	...and jumps from platform where crates were situated...
	2:55	Cut - Another angle - Tom in midair.
	2:55 1/2	He disappears out of frame, as Camera pans to ground and shadows beneath.
	2:57	S running across top of building.
	2:58 1/2	He lowers himself to crouching position, still moving toward ladder.
CLx #2	3:05	Cut - Down Shot, as Tom moves into frame.
MS2/61, A (+3)	3:05 2/3	He kneels, quickly looking up in S's direction.
14-4 CLy (5) *8 FREE*	3:07 1/3	Cut - His PoV of ladder. Nothing is visible.
(8+)	3:09 1/3	Cut back - Previous Angle as he surveys entire roof.
(13+)	3:12 1/3	Cut - Far left-hand corner of sign as S's head appears.
15	3:13 1/3	S begins edging over, to get between sign and building.
23+2FR	3:18 1/2	Cut - Down Shot - Tom, still looking at right-hand side of sign.
28 -4FR	3:21	Cut back - S.
29	3:21 2/3	Raising slightly, he jumps...
30	3:22 1/2	...and disappears behind sign, leaving only his hands visible, hanging onto top.
32+	3:23 2/3	He begins to appear intermittently at top, going hand-over-hand toward left-hand side of sign.
41+2	3:29 1/3	Cut - Tom - Still watching wrong side of sign.
45+3	3:31 2/3	Cut to Shot Up - Left-hand edge as S inches his way along toward end of sign.
51+	3:35 1/2	Reaching the edge, he leans over and grabs large pipe, and, bracing himself, pulls toward it.

(cont'd.)

128

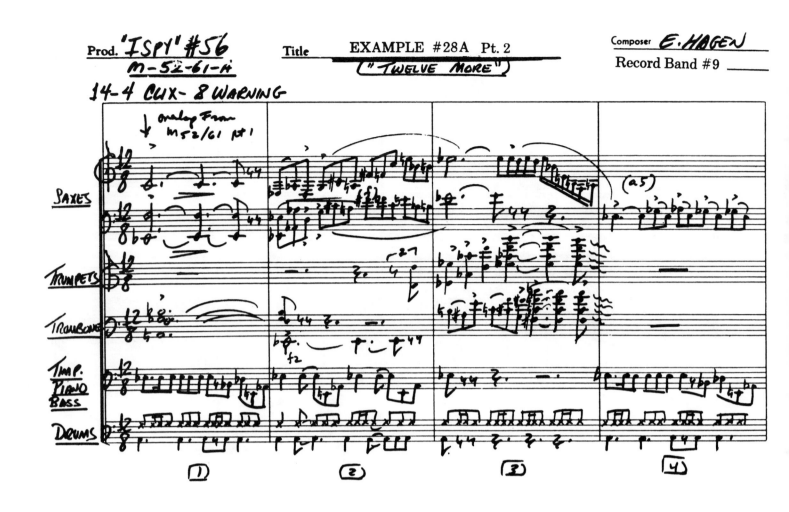

M-26/31 (P. 3.)

1:34 1/2	Tonia: " NO, WE ARE NOT, IT WILL BE A SEMINAR, A DISCUSSION PERIOD." (Ends 1:38 1/2)
1:39 1/2	Scott: " O.K., ANYTHING YOU SAY - 'COURSE YA KNOW YOU'RE NOT GONNA FOOL THE ANTS. " (Ends 1:42)
1:42	Cut to Two-Shot as they start away with cart.
1:42 1/2	She protests in Italian about his haste: " SE---, SEE---." (Ends 1:44 1/2)
1:47	They start carefully to carry cart down a long flight of steps.

End Clx. → *1:54 3/4*

1:51 1/3	Cut to Start of Rec/3 as Scott & Tonia are coming down Spanish Steps toward camera from a L.S.
1:56	Start Dissolve.

M26/31A → ①(1:58) *OVERLAP*

Full In on M.S. Scott & Tonia sitting on wall by river.

⊕ *2:04*

2:06	She hops down from wall and beckons him to come along.
2:09 2/3	Start Dissolve.
2:11 2/3	Full In as S. & T. approach shop window.

⊕ *2:14 2/3*

2:15	They stop to look.
2:18	While she bends to look at something, Scott disappears into the shop.

⊕ *2:18 1/3*

2:21	She looks up but doesn't see Scott.
2:22 1/3	She looks about.

⊕ *2:22 2/3*

2:24 2/3   Scott appears from behind.

⊕ *2:26 2/3*

2:27 2/3   He presents her with a silk scarf.

2:29   He places it around her neck as she becomes happily embarrassed.

⊕ *2:30 2/3*
⊕ *2:34 2/3*

2:38 2/3   She places a hand-kiss on his lips.

(2:39 1/3)   Start Dissolve

2:41 1/3   Full In on a Full Shot of S. & T. playing a kind of 'towel-tag' on the steps of a large building.

⊕ *2:43 1/3*

2:43 2/3   He siezes her around waist-both very happy.

⊕ *2:45 1/3*

2:47   They sit on steps-she in his arms as he starts nuzzling up.

(2:49 1/3)   Start Dissolve

(cont'd.)

130

EXAMPLE #29 (Cont.)

I SPY #43

M-26/31 (P. 4.)

2:51 1/3   Full In on a very bustling scene of pedestrians.

2:53   Camera starts moving in closer through the corwd.

2:55 1/2   Camera stops Med. Close on Scott & Tonia in a
            tight smooching clinch-completely oblivious of
⊕2:59   the passing crowd that is also oblivious of them.

3:03   Start Dissolve.

3:05   She says: " I DON'T KNOW, YOU'VE DONE SOMETHING
            TO ME--I FEEL SO NEW. " (Ends 3:09)

3:09   Cut to C.U. Scott-really smitten.

3:10 2/3   Scott answers: "BECAUSE YOU WERE 'NEW' ALL
            THE TIME." (Ends 3:12 2/3)

3:15 2/3   They start to move slowly in for another big kiss.

3:18 1/3   They contact in big kiss.

3:21 1/3   Cut to Reverse Angle C.U. on Tonia-nuzzling
            and loving this kind of attention.
⊕3:22⅓
3:22 2/3   She says, Happily gasping: "OH! THANK YOU, THANK
            YOU! DIO TE BENE DICA." (Ends 3:26 2/3)

3:27   Cut to M.C. Two-Shot.

3:27 1/2   Scott: "DON'T THANK ME, O.K.? JUST DON'T THANK
⊕3:29⅓   ME!" (Ends 3:31 1/2)

3:31 1/2   He moves away toward door as though caught in
            something he's undecided about.

3:35   Closes door behind him.

3:35 1/3   Cut to CU Tonia-perplexed about S.'s sudden change

3:42   She looks-a bit sadly now-down at the scarf he
            gave her.

3:43 2/3   Start Dissolve

3:45 2/3   Music Seques to M-33 as picture Full In on C.U.
            bartender's hands serving two glasses on top
            of bar.

TOTAL TIME 3:45 2/3

Prod. "I SPY" #43
M-26-31-A

Title EXAMPLE #29A Pt. 2

Composer E. HAGEN
Arranger PAGE 1.

Record Band #10

Prod. _____   Title **EXAMPLE #29A Pt. 2 (Cont.)**   Composer _____
Arranger *PAGE 2.*

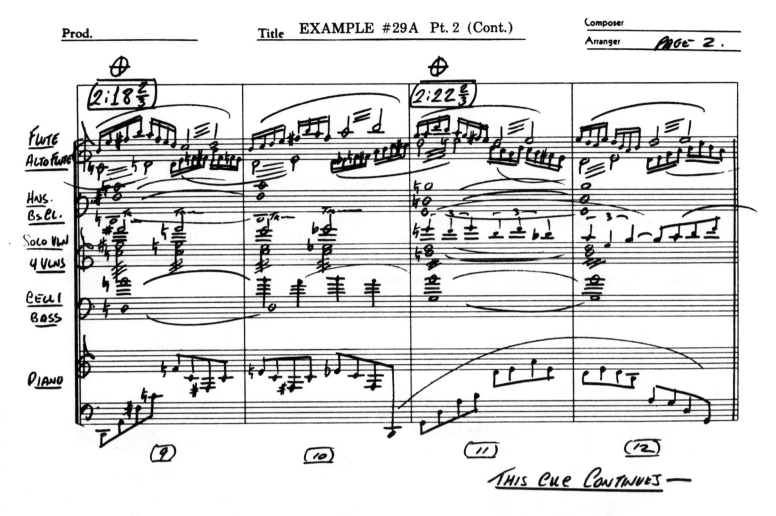

THIS CUE CONTINUES —

Example 29 —The overlap within a cue from a free timing to free timing.

This cue, "I SPY" #43—M26/31, had a dissolve at 1:58 that changed the character of the scene from gay and bright to very romantic. The cue started in a 9 frame click track and had to meet the overlap at 1:58 seconds. The example picks up the scene at the 286th click; the downbeat of bar 74. In order to make the rallentando into the next section, M26/31-A, the clicks were stopped at 1:54 3/4 seconds (click #304 1/2) and the overlap was accomplished in free timing with a streamer catching 1:58 seconds. From an orchestration stand point, the downbeat of the overlap bar, bar 81, which sustained, is exactly the same as the downbeat of the incoming cue M26/31-A. This section is notated to start at 1:58 seconds of the original start mark. It has been previously mentioned that an overlap allows you to reset the orchestra. You will notice that in the first section, M26/31, there is an accordion written in this cue. In the second section, he goes to piano. The slight addition of weight created by the entrance of the E flat contrabass clarinet and the harp in the beginning of the new section, M26/31-A, serves identically the same orchestra function as if there were no overlap involved. The reason to break was that a change in recording technique was desired for the second section. The first part was fast and bright and recorded with no artificial reverberation. The second section was romantic and involved a lush kind of string writing that called for some reverb. This not only gave the engineer a chance to make a recording adjustment that would have been touchy if the cue had gone straight through, but it also allowed the accordion to change to piano, and gave the orchestra a rest from the fast and somewhat difficult first section.

Example 30 —The overlap within a cue from free timing to a click track—"I SPY" #52-M15/21.

This cue was dramatic in context and at :38 1/3rd seconds a sharp move started a visual fight. The first part of this cue was in free timing to picture; the overlap at :38 1/3rd allowed a use of a click track to catch the fight action, a change of orchestra set up, and a change of recording technique. In this instance, the sweep up to a short note in the strings in the outgoing section is matched orchestra-wise by the note on which they land being trilled in the beginning of the new section. This simple device achieved the overlap and allowed the new section, M15/21-A, to continue as though it was recorded in one sequence from the beginning.

135

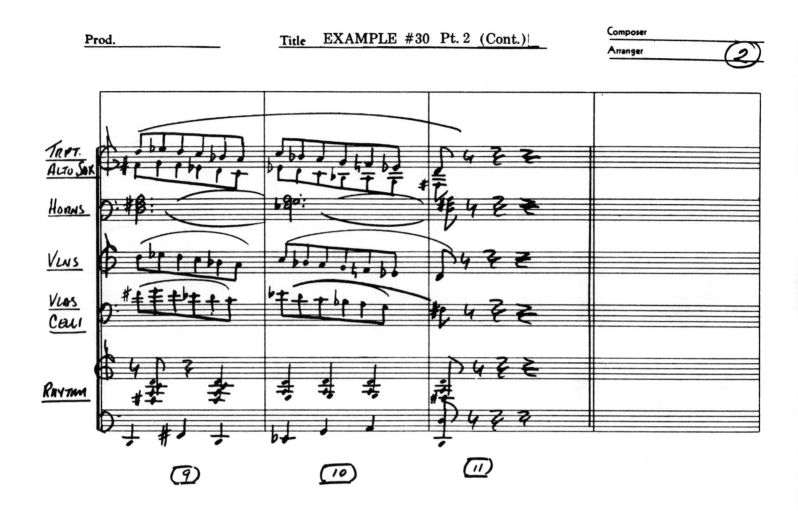

Example 31 —The overlap within a cue from a click track to free timing—"I SPY" #11—
M-32.

This particular cue not only demonstrates the overlap from a click track to free timing but takes up the subject of the long dissolve. As the cue sheet indicates, the first part of the scene involves the two principals getting into a car and driving into the Japanese countryside. At :45 seconds there is the start of a 10 foot dissolve. The first part of the cue—M32—was handled with a click track. At :45 seconds, the start of the overlap—M32-A—the strings reached an open fifth structure that held to click #111—:51 2/3rds. —the "full in" of the dissolve. The incoming cue—M32-A—started with a harp (Quasi Koto) and Japanese Damar bells. Starting at :45 seconds the two tracks were running simultaneously. The string setting started to die out from :45 seconds on as the Japanese effect came in and took over. The two tracks lingered together momentarily and musically dissolved into the Japanese setting of alto flute, "mandolin" piano, harp, and light percussion. This orchestral setting carried the burden of the walk through the Tsugo Shrine and was later developed into a full orchestral setting as the second scene built.

*   *   *

EXAMPLE #31

11-2 CY   M32 -T2   I SPY #11   158'
8 FREE   M32A -T1   M32 St MK -138'
                        M-32 PLAYIN-PICTURE   M32A St MK -206'

.00   F.I. from - K.& T. walking out to car-
               on their way for a picnic.

M32A
NOTE ON   .07-1/3   K. opens car door for her.
DUBD
L-STGS   .09-2/3   She gets in.
C-W.WONY   .11-1/3   He starts around car.
R-RHY   .14 1/2   ..opens door..

               .16-1/3   ..and gets in

               .19   Starts car.

               .22   As they start out, start 8 foot dissolve to
                              freeway - The car moving along.

97th CY   .27-1/3   Full In - Camera pans with car.
M32A   START OVERLAP
               .45-1/3   Start 10 foot dissolve to shrine in "redwoods"-
                              Camera panning down.

111th CY   .51-2/3   Full In - Camera starts to pan across
               END OVERLAP
               .56   We see K. & T. walking to shrine.

               .57-1/3   Camera ends pan - M.L.S. of them as they
                              approach

               .59-3/3
               1:05-2/3   T: "I give you Tsugo Shrine, to be in it is to
                              be renewed, replenished. You know, it's been
                              exactly like that for 450 years? I've photo-
               1:12-2/3   graphed it a dozen times, and each time it
                              seems different to me." (ends 1:19-2/3)
               1:19-2/3

               1:27-1/3
               1:28-1/3   Start 10foot dissolve to C.S. of "monkey
                              carvings"

               1:35   Full In - Camera is pulling back.

               1:43   We see K. looking at them -

               1:44 1/2   --and T. standing beside him.

               1:44-2/3   T; "The carvings tell a story, it goes from
                              there, --"

(continued)

EXAMPLE #31 (Cont.)

PROD. *"I SPY" #11*   CUE *M-32*   TITLE_____   COMP. *EARLE HAGEN*   PAGE *1*

"THE PICNIC"

11-2 CLICK TRACK

EXAMPLE #31 (Cont.)

Prod. "ISPY" #11
M-32-A - "NIKKO

EXAMPLE #31   Pt. 2

Composer E. HAGEN

Record Band #11

EXAMPLE #31 Pt. 2 (Cont.)

These examples cover the various overlaps within a cue. They serve to demonstrate that you can have the freedom to split a cue using any mechancial procedures whatsoever. All you need to split a cue is a physical or dramatic reason. Obviously, if you can record hard cues in short takes, the problems of going for extra takes are not as severe as having to make a whole five minute sequence over and over again. In order to do this properly and not suffer musically, you must have a picture sequence that allows you this freedom. This particular example was a cue that was over five minutes long and the hardest part of it was the first 45 seconds!

There are many other necessary uses for the overlap. They do not involve splitting cues, however, and actually serve the purpose of segues.

#2. Overlaps from cue to cue.

So far, we have examined only overlaps dealing with the splitting of a cue.

The major portion of the overlaps with which we deal are generally in the nature of cue to cue. Once again, all of the previously discussed methods can be used. Click to clicks; clicks to free timing; free timing to clicks; and free timing to free timing. The very nature of an overlap taking place on a cue-to-cue basis presupposes that there is a visual reason for the change of cue, and that there is a marked difference in the sound of the music. In making an overlap inside of a cue, we seek to preserve the continuity so as not to make the overlap noticeable. In making overlaps on a cue-to-cue basis, we go in exactly the opposite direction and call attention to the fact that there is a noticeable change in the music. The most common example would be to go from scoring to source. Books of examples could be printed, but the fact of the matter is that there are really only two things to consider. First—do you want the transition to be smooth? Second—do you want the transition to "bump" in and be noticeable?

In the first instance, you might be playing a principle theme in a scoring mode and then dissolve to your principal actors having a drink in a cocktail lounge. If you wanted your transition to be smooth, you would try to time your scoring cue so that you could sustain or cross over to your new cue in such a way as to continue your thematic material in a completely different character. Say that you are scoring a warm scene with a string and woodwind setting, and in the middle of the dissolve you start a new cue with a solo piano continuing the thematic thread. You might consider this as a split cue, but it really isn't. The dissolve is the key. It provides you with a visual necessity to make a change of musical location and character. The fact that you might continue your thematic material does not negate the fact that these are still two separate cues. You could just as easily go to a new piece of material for the incoming scene. The principal point to observe is that while there is no necessity for orchestration duplication, there is a necessity for key relationship. Naturally, the reverse holds true. You could go from a dance band cue in a nightclub sequence to a scoring scene in a key-related manner and make the transition very smooth by the careful use of key relationships.

In this day of fast cutting technique—where direct cuts are used instead of dissolves–the problems of crossovers are harder to handle than in a straight scoring cue, or source cue, that does not cross into the incoming cue. The problem of where and how to get out of these film traps has yet to be solved. The direct cut can be treated like a dissolve, and the music can sustain on the cut. If the scene allows, you can get out on the cut. These are sticky dilemmas and can't be solved by any formula. Each case is different and you have to make up your mind as to the solution.

In the second instance, that of "bumping" two cues together, the very thing that you do not want is a key relationship. If you are working with short dissolves, it is practical to come to a conclusion at the start of the dissolve, and let the incoming cue "bump in" in a totally unrelated manner. If you were going from a scoring sequence to a discotheque, the more raucous the incoming cue, the better. This technique should be used wherever you wish to feel the transition immediately. The bulk of these kinds of overlaps are carried by the source music on one side of the dissolve or the other. Scoring-to-dance band, dance band-to-dance band, and dance band-to-scoring lend themselves best to the "bump" method. When you are crossing from scoring to scoring, you want your transitions to have continuity. You can have tremendous changes in the values of the music through a dissolve, but to bump them together would make them sound like someone had pasted two pieces of track together. We will go into more detail on these problems when we approach scoring from the psychological aspect.

CHAPTER 13
OVERLAY TRACKS

Example 32 illustrates the use of an overlay track. The cue sheet tells you that a flamenco guitarist is performing on camera. Against the flamenco guitarist, a dramatic scene is being played where a principal actor is being put under hypnosis by means of a light being flashed in his eyes with a mirror. The device that was set up earlier in the picture for the mirror was a haze track. It was recorded with echo return only and produced a hazy, hypnotic sound. When the actor is visually put under hypnosis and instructed to kill his best friend, the haze track starts. The haze track and the flamenco guitar track run simultaneously and musically are completely unrelated. You have two independent music tracks going together—each adding its connotation to the scene. At the point where a fight starts, the guitarist, in reaction to the scene, stops playing—and so does the haze track. The purpose of the overlay track was to continue the thought that the actor was under hypnosis. The flamenco music was active and florid—the haze track was passive and simple. Although they were not related in any way, they both worked and produced an effective sequence musically for an effective sequence visually. Because the sequence was long—1:41—and because the haze pattern was only a two bar pattern that was repeated, a total of 10 bars of the pattern was recorded. This was made into a loop and an overlong print was made from this loop. As you can see by the score, there was an instruction to the cutter to cut the track off at 1:41. The whole recording process took less than 45 seconds, and we wound up with an effective double track sequence.

Example 33 shows another kind of overlay. This was determined by an impossible physical notation problem. A bar breakdown was made first with all of the pertinent details on it. The sequence was one where a shuttered light is being flashed on and off in the actors eyes in an effort to put him under hypnotic suggestion. A background haze was set in the orchestra as the light was first flashed on. If you examine the notations of where the light flashed on and off, you realize that to try to write the effect rhythmically would involve divisions of beats that would be practically impossible to play. The problem of doing a trick like this is that once you commit yourself to the concept of catching the lights, you have to catch them all—and they must fit exactly to be effective. The solution was simple once the problem was recognized as being complex. The basic orchestra background was recorded overlong. At the end of the cut you will see a bar marked M25-A—Overlay. This effect in muted brass, piano, harp, and cymbal, was made ten times. There were ten flashes of light involved in the cue. Each one of the effects was cut in exactly where the action took place. When they were balanced with the basic orchestra background, the effect was a single track that caught every light flash—exactly! The effect of the previous example involving the guitar track was a real double track. The second was a single track effect with all of the film obligations met. Both were accomplished by overlays.

EXAMPLE #32

I SPY #28

Start 278,
248'

MAKE LOOP OF HAZE TRK + REPRINT
:00

M-44   OVERLAY TO M-43 - PICTURE
       (Check against record)

(FLAMENCO GUITARIST PLAYING UNTIL FIGHT STARTS PIC)

Start after cut to Vanessa's hands holding compact on <u>flash</u>

:02   Cut 2-shot Vanessa & K with reflection on K's face

:03 1/3   Vanessa reacts to see if S is watching

:03 2/3   Cut - S is looking away

:05 2/3   2-shot Vanessa & K

:07   Vanessa glances down at her hands - reflection still on K

⊕ :09
:10   K blinks

:11   Cut - the doctor and heavie watching

:13 1/3   2-shot - Vanessa & K

:15 1/3   Shot - S looking at K and Vanessa

:16 1/3   S rubs jaw pensively

⊕ :17 1/2 2-shot Vanessa & K
:18
:19   K is blinking again

:21 1/3   K glances at champagne

:24   K grabs champagne in bucket

:25 1/2   Cut - master as K pulls out champagne

:27 2/3   He pours in his glass

:30 1/3   He tries to pour in S glass but S puts hands over glass

:30 2/3   S: "NO"

:31 1/2   Cut single of S

:32 1/3   2-shot - K still trying to pour in S glass

:34   S, o.s.: "C'MON"

:36 1/3   K: "WHAT'S THE MATTER?"

(continued)

EXAMPLE #32 (Cont.)

I SPY #28

M-44 (page 2)

:37   Cut - S: "NO THANK YOU"

:38   2-shot - Vanessa & K: "OH, THAT'S RIGHT --
           I'VE NEVER KNOWN MY MAN TO BE IMPURE --
           I'VE TRIED FOR MANY YEARS TO FORCE UPON
           HIM SOME OF THE OTHER WAY OF IMPURE & EVIL
           PEOPLE LIKE MYSELF, BUT IT JUST DOESN'T
           WORK -- IT'S PURE"

:50 1/3   Cut S smiling to above

:52 2/3   Cut 2-shot Vanessa & K

:56 2/3   Cut S

:57 1/3   2-shot Vanessa & K

:58   K shouts out: "MY MAN IS PURE, I SAY TO YOU!"
           (ends 1:00 2/3)

:59 1/3   Cut 2-shot Doctor & heavie

1:00 2/3   Cut shot of S - shaking head no

1:02   2-shot Vanessa & K

1:03 2/3   Cut shot of S

1:04 1/3   S: "C'MON, WATCH YOURSELF, DUKE.   YOU'RE HITTIN'
           THE SAUCE A LITTLE TOO HARD." (Ends 1:07 1/2)

1:07 1/2   2-shot Vanessa & K: "C'MON MAN, HAVE A LITTLE
           OF THIS GOOD JUICE HERE." (Ends 1:10)

1:10 1/2   Shot - S: "NO, DON'T PUT THAT STUFF IN MY GLASS."
           (ends 1:12 1 2)

1:12 1/2   2-shot Vanessa & K - K jerkily starts to pour
           the champagne over S's arm - K: "THERE WE GO A
           LITTLE THERE"

1:18 1/2   Cut shot S disgusted

1:20   2-shot Vanessa & K: "AND DOWN THERE AND SOME
           THERE AND SOME RIGHT HERE" - as K pours champagne
           out on S's arm

1:25   K has emptied bottle and places it on table

1:28   He looks up at S with deceit in eyes

continued....

Record Band #12

Prod. "ISPY" #28
M-44

Title   EXAMPLE #32 (Cont.)

Composer E. HAGEN
Arranger

EXAMPLE #33

I SPY #28

19-0 d̄ 8 FREE

St MK 494'

M 25   PICTURE   5l4 ft.

:00   The Dr.'s assistants have dressed K. & are leading him
           across room.
           Music starts as we hear the light switch & see the light
           flash on K.'s face.

:01 2/3   The assistant walks K. over to the light which is flashing
           on & off.

           Check against bar breakdown.

→ :16 1/3   Music ends.

DONT CUT OFF Total Time - :16 1/3

M 25 (T1)

M 25 A   OVERLAYS   T 1

CUT iN !!!

*Fx NOTE   TRY TO CLEAN OUT
                SHUTTER NOISE ON
                OPENING— (LEAVE IN FOR
                                CLOSING)*

Record Band #13

Prod. "I SPY" #28
M-25

Title   EXAMPLE #33 (Cont.)

Composer E. HAGEN
Arranger

19.0 CLIX - 4 BARS 4/4 = 12⅔ SEC. METRO = APPROX. 75   8 FREE TO D.B. B-1.

M-25-A - OVERLAY

(PLAY 10 TIMES)

CHAPTER 14
DOUBLE TRACKING

Double tracking is a useful device if not overdone. A montage scene of a crowded street of night clubs lends itself to double tracking. Actually, you can use more than two tracks simultaneously. If the shot were moving down the street, you might have several tracks of different combinations and tunes, unrelated, overlapping each other to give the effect of passing by many different sources of literal music.

Double tracking can also be effective dramatically. A case in point was a sequence in a picture where a church organ was playing a mass. A killer was being stalked through the church and a bass ostinato pattern was laid under the organ music in the low end of the orchestra and eventually built to a tremendous pitch as the killer broke out into the street.

Clicks are extremely helpful in double tracking especially if you wish the music to be oriented to the picture. It isn't necessary to have the two or more tracks fit together. As a matter of fact, the more independence they have from each other, the more you hear them and the more the trick pays off. One word of caution: these effects should be worked out musically. You are looking for confusion of sound when you go to double tracking. Make sure that it is organized confusion.

EXAMPLE #34

I SPY #13   439 ft

M - 14 SOURCE PICTURE (?)

.00	CROSS FROM M-13 . ON START OF DISS. TO F.S. NITE EXT. THE HOUSE.
.02	FULL IN.
.03-½	CAMERA STARTS TO PAN DOWN.
.08	HOLDS ON F.S. OF TENNIS COURT.
.09-1/3	KID SNEAKS OUT ON TENNIS COURT, CARRYING HIS BAG OF GOODIES.
.21	HE STOPS BY NET AND LOOKS UP TOWARDS HOUSE.
.23-1/3	HE STARTS OVER TO CENTER OF COURT.
.27	PUTS BAG DOWN...
.29	...AND STARTS TO OPEN IT...
.30-2/3	...BRINGS OUT HIS TOOLS...
.35	...AND STARTS TO WORK.
.35-1/3	CUT. TO INT. PARTY GOING ON.

EXAMPLE #34 (Cont.)

.36-2/3 DIAL. STARTS. S. TALKING TO A COUPLE.

.56-1/3 WE SEE K. AND MISS DIMBULB.

.59-½ DIAL. STARTS BETWEEN THEM ABOUT TENNIS AND SHE
DOESN'T LIKE IT, ETC.

1.37-1/3 CUT TO EXT. THEKID'S HANDS PICKING UP THE MINE ON
THE TENNIS COURT. (SOURCE WILL CONTINUE) O.S.

Long pause.

1.44 HE PLANTS THE MINE...

1.46-½ *Start PK II* ...ARMS IT...

1.48-2/3 ...AND BEGINS COVERING IT UP.

1.49-½ CUT TO INT. THE PARTY.

1.53 CUT TO K. AND MISS DIMBULB.

1.53-1/3 DIAL. BETWEEN THEM.

2.00 MR. OKARA ENTERS AND TALKS TO K. HE INTRODUCES
TOSHIO, K. INTRO'S MISS D. THEY ASK TO BORROW K.

2.43-2/3 K. TELLS HER TO LET THEM BORROW HIM. HE'LL PAY
HER BACK.

2.49-1/3 SHE AGREES.

2.51-2/3 THE MEN EXIT.

3.02 MR. OK. TELLS K. ABOUT TOSHIO'S TENNIS RECORD.

3.09 MR. OK. INTRODUCES K. TO COLONEL ALLEN AND THEY
TALK. END SOURSE ANYWHERE BETWEEN HERE AND 3.28.

MAKE OVERLONG IN FRONT AND NATURAL ENDING.

Total time (minimum) 3.09

THE MECHANICS AND VOCABULARY
OF
FILM COMPOSITION

EXAMPLE #34
DOUBLE TRACKING

As you can see by the cue sheet, "I SPY" #13—M14, this scene dissolves into a full shot of a house in which a cocktail party is taking place. As the camera pans down at :03 1/2 seconds, you pick up a kid sneaking onto a tennis court to plant a mine. Track 1 is a small combo playing the party. Track 2 is a low register menacing sound that is re-recorded in close perspective with Track #1 leaking through to keep the party alive while the kid does his dirty work. At click #48 minus (4 frms) we cut to the interior and the party music goes right on in a closer perspective. Track #2 disappears at this point and is not heard until later in this cue. Both of these tracks were recorded to the same click from the same start. Track #2 is deliberately dissonant and *not* related to Track #1 in key structure or character. This grinding difference between the two concurrently running tracks is what maintains their identity and keeps both of them alive. When you cut to the interior and the dramatic sounding track disappears, the ear naturally follows the combo into the atmosphere of the party.

EXAMPLE #34   Track 1/Track 2   Record Band #14

EXAMPLE #34 (Cont.)

THE MECHANICS AND VOCABULARY
OF
FILM COMPOSITION

Double tracking is usually done to separate two visual ideas by having two separate musical ideas working at the same time. There is, however, another kind of double tracking. This is where you take some exotic instrument, or group of instruments, and add a new orchestral background for dramatic purposes. Record Band 34A will help illustrate this kind of double tracking.

While working with the I SPY television company in the Greek islands, I had an occasion to buy a reel of ethnic music that was broadcast from the radio station on the island of Rhodes. It was my policy to pick up ethnic music wherever we were traveling and mix it into background situations such as market places, arcades and restaurants. Because the show was shot entirely on location and was both a travelogue and action anthology, the use of ethnic music helped fix the geographic location.

The tape I purchased on Rhodes was P. D. material that was performed by local people. Some of the tracks were stunning. The most effective of them all was a clarinet cadenza that lasted some five minutes. A bass, cymbalom and guitar played a G-minor chord and the clarinet played for a full breath in the lowest register. When he stopped to breathe, the guitar and bass played a G-diminished chord and a G-minor chord. With the cymbalom tremoloing a G, the clarinet started another cadenza a notch up. They kept doing this until the clarinet had covered the entire range of the instrument, up to the B-flat and down to the low G.

The performance was sensational and I marked on my notes, "double track." I had no idea where I was going to use it, but I knew that if the picture opportunity arose, I was going to take advantage of it.

Along came a Greek show called "Laya." In it was a sequence where a young thief was sent to go through Bob Culp and Bill Cosby's room to verify for a foreign embassy that they were American spies. The sequence was very stylized in the way it was shot. All of it was done with a hand-held camera — in tight and very dark. The thief did everything with a knife: opening drawers and throwing the contents on the floor, turning over books and letters while moving from one room to another. In the middle of this, Culp returns. He sees the condition of the room and knows that someone else is there. The thief jumps him and a fight ensues — also very stylized with the close hand-held camera in the semi-darkness. Furniture is broken, lamps are shattered and, finally after throwing the knife at Culp and missing, the thief escapes.

The minute I saw it, I went to the producer, Sheldon Leonard, and told him that I had an idea. I said I would like him to take out all of the sound effects with the exception of Culp unlocking the door that let the thief know there was someone else in the room. He asked me if the music was going to underline the fight. I replied that it would imply it only. I didn't attempt to tell him what I had in mind, only that it would be theatrical as hell. Having had a close association with him for a good long time, he said okay.

I dug out my clarinet track, took it down to the recording stage and with a variable speed oscillator dummy brought it up to pitch. The original track was quite flat. My music editor and I then took three copies of the whole track and cut them to fit the picture. We never cut into the middle of a cadenza, but used each segment in its entirety, skipping some, gapping others — in general, cutting the track so that the clarinet by itself really scored the scene. I made no attempt to take down what the clarinet was playing. All I was interested in was the time where he stopped playing and at what time he started again. I had a reference tape made and, with the cue sheet giving me the action, picked a click track and wrote the orchestra accompaniment.

The end result is on Record Band Ex. 34A.

Was it worth the trouble? Yes! It's always worth some extra effort if you can make a theatrical effect that helps the picture.

CHAPTER 15
SWEETENER TRACKS

The last device to be discussed in the mechanical part of this book is the use of the Sweetener*.

A sweetener is any effect that is not recorded with the original track, but added later. In the previous example of the light flashes, the musical effect was really a sweetener to the original track.

The sweetener is very useful whenever you have problems in recording. For example, if you needed a chime note in the middle of a large tutti, it would be better to leave the chime out in the original recording and do it at the end of the date as a sweetener. It could be recorded wild and cut in. Exotic effects that are soft in character can be recorded as sweeteners.

Some film recording studios have a low tolerance for percussion. If you had a marching band sequence and needed a good crisp percussion sound, you would probably be better off to record the band to clicks to provide them with the beat, and then record the percussion section separately and combine them in whatever perspective you desire.

If you wanted a solo with a lot of reverb, and yet didn't want the orchestra to swim on you, you could record the orchestra track first and then add your solo with whatever degree of echo you felt was necessary. Keep the sweetener in mind. It can be very effective and get you through a lot of difficult recording situations.

See Example. #32

THE SUMMARY OF THE MECHANICS

It would be presumptuous to assume that any text or group of texts could present every kind of problem and its solution. For every problem solved today, a new one appears tomorrow. The purpose of Book I has been to put into your hands some of the equipment, procedures and language of everyday film music techniques. It is the idea of this book to orient you to the questions that arise and the methods of answering them. Somewhere in the past 15 chapters, almost every mechanical difficulty that is familiar has been examined. If the solution to a specific problem that may arise has not been covered by a specific answer, the usage of the procedures or combinations of procedures should help you find the solution. Too many times, in the face of a rough situation, the composer has the tendency to overestimate the problem and look for a complicated answer. More often than not, the solution for a seemingly complex problem is simple. Try to solve the difficult situations with the easiest methods available. Use the trick solution when no other will suffice.

You should by now have a pretty fair knowledge of what the mechanical procedures are about, and how to handle them. You have also been introduced to the language of film music and music cutting. We will continue to build that language as we proceed.

*See glossary

*   *   *

BOOK II

THE PSYCHOLOGY
OF
CREATING MUSIC FOR FILMS

THE PSYCHOLOGY OF CREATING MUSIC
FOR FILMS

A SYMPOSIUM ON THE COMPOSERS VIEWS TOWARDS THE PSYCHOLOGY

In order to establish the vague area that exists when the psychology of film music is discussed, the author conducted an experiment with established and recognized film composers, covering a wide field of experience and technique. The questions were loaded. They were designed to create chain reactions that would cause the composer to do some soul searching and force him to enter the never-never land of musical and theatrical philosophy. The composers who were interviewed were: Alfred Newman, Jerrald Goldsmith, Hugo Friedhofer, Quincy Jones, and Lalo Schifrin. The dialogue that took place between the author and these distinguished composers is presented for inspection. The questions were:

1. *What contribution do you feel that the composer must make for his film?*

2. *How do you determine where music shall start and stop in your film?*

3. *What special treatment, if any, do you make for playing music under dialogue?*

4. *To what extent does the picture dictate the necessities and style of the musical score?*

QUESTION #1: *What contribution do you feel that the composer must make for the film?*

ANSWER FROM MR. NEWMAN

Quote:

"This question seems at first glance to be elementary, whereas in fact it is quite complex since many factors are involved.

Every film has (or should have) its personal style, mood, character and philosophy to which the composer must address himself if he is to serve as an effective contributor.

In my judgement, music for films is, in a broad sense, a third dimension—a unifying element, in key with the film's dramatic and stylistic content. In this context, the composer may choose a literal or an abstract approach, according to his own taste and judgement.

I also believe that film music is more closely related to the opera and ballet, than 'absolute' music.

While I don't think that a score need be totally subliminal, its 'voice' should blend, objectively and subjectively, with all the elements inherent in the film.

In broad general terms, music should contribute to, and be in harmony with the varying moods, style, and philosophy of the total picture."

ANSWER FROM MR. SCHIFRIN

Quote:

"Well, I think that unless the film is planned by the film maker not to have any music in it— as an example, the British film, THE HILL, in which there was no music at all—unless this is planned, as I have said, the music is part of the audio-visual counterpoint. That means that the music is planned to bring a counterline to what is visually and dramatically going on in the film. There are many reasons—you want the audience to be involved, and sometimes the music can be subliminal. I particularly feel that the best for the film is the one that is less self-conscious. It creates a sort of subliminal enhancement of what is dramatically and visually going on, and it creates the perfect psychological climate for the audience to be absorbed by what is going on in the scene."

THE PSYCHOLOGY OF CREATING MUSIC
FOR FILMS

QUESTION #1: *What contribution do you feel that the composer must make for the film?*

ANSWER FROM MR. FRIEDHOFER

Quote:

"His contribution is to give a certain smoothness of continuity to a medium that is by its very nature jumpy and choppy, what with its cuts, its dissolves, its changes of mood and pace. He can, without smoothing out to the point where it becomes utterly bland, he can sort of cement or glue these dramatic elements together with his judicious use of scoring."

ANSWER FROM MR. JONES

Quote:

"We try to create a fabric for the picture. In a sense, that's what it feels like to me—an additional emotional third dimension. I sometimes try to find a different approach—but I always try to select the proper emotional fabric for a film. That, combined with showmanship, is probably personal with each composer. It's finding the X element in a film and surrounding it with that certain unknown 'something'."

ANSWER FROM MR. GOLDSMITH

Quote:

"I feel that there is no set formula for writing music for a film. I think that music should make a comment on what is going on, what the dramatic implications are—I don't feel that is should mimic what is being done—it should make a separate comment on what is being shown on the screen. We should write music that underlines the basic emotions of the film, the story, the drama—we should tie together sequences—a lot of times we are called upon to save a picture, which is impossible. I have always said that a bad film was never saved by good music, but an awful amount of bad music has been saved by a good film.

There are times when you must strain to say something because the picture, the story, the drama, leaves you so flat. I think that all we can do is make a true, honest, sincere comment on what the man who wrote it, and the man who directed it, and the actors who portrayed the characters, were trying to say."

QUESTION #2. *How do you determine where music shall start and stop in your film?*

ANSWER FROM MR. NEWMAN

Quote:

"I don't think that this question can be answered with sweeping generalizations. The determination as to where to start and stop music would necessarily evolve from the dramatic content and style of a *specific* film, after very careful deliberation.

This is an area of utmost importance. It is in this area that the lurking pitfall of intrusion lies. Introducing music (or for that matter stopping it) ineptly, can destroy the dramatic concept of any given picture.

In my own experience, I have found many ways of avoiding these pitfalls. I will try to cite a few possibilities. (These are naturally hypothetical situations).

A simple but effective device is to start a musical scene over an arresting shot such as a huge head close up of a principle character for instance or a relevant piece of action from which the music would evolve. This music could stop on an ensuing scene which, let us say, would be a roaring train with appropriate sound effects. Conversely, the sound effects would evolve from the music which preceded, thus leaving the auditor with a sense of dramatic continuity. This sort of device dispels the pitfall of intrusion, both at the starting point *and* the stopping point and provides a subliminal unification of *both* scenes.

Another example: There is always the gunshot, to be sure. (Editor's Note: This refers to a later example). Since in my opinion the 'Stinger' has had its day, I have found it more effective to start music after the sound of the shot.

Let us assume that the gunfire is the beginning of a shoot-out between mounted men and is full of the sounds of shooting, and galloping horses.

The action and sound effects furnish an excellent counterpoint to music which could be highly dramatic, expressing the emotions of the characters involved rather than merely accompanying the speed of the action. I think this approach gives us the opportunity to write more meaningful music.

But how and where to stop is another problem.

Since all of this is hypothetical, let us say the afore-mentioned scene dissolves or cuts to a rural landscape.

Tranquility prevails. Heard only are the sounds of nature. Should we play a pastorale, in sharp contrast to the blood and thunder which preceded it? I think not! More effective, I think is the use of natures sounds in this case, without any music to intrude upon the tranquility.

Mr. Newman answer continued.

There are, of course, many more devices in this area.

Briefly summarized, I would say that the pitfall of intrusion should always be avoided."

QUESTION #2. *How do you determine where music shall start and stop in your film?*

ANSWER FROM MR. SCHIFRIN

Quote:

"I don't have pre-conceptions or theories about that—I resolve each problem as it comes. It's very difficult to make general theories about this because each movie is an entity of its own. In order to answer your question specifically, again I say, it all depends on the style of the movie. For instance, in television, there is a tendency to start a cue every time that there is no dialogue and there is action, and when dialogue comes in—the music goes out. This is the sort of cliche that has become routine. Most of the time, I must admit, it works, but I think that the creative composer might consider different situations in which he might put music under dialogue and no music under action. There are incredibly infinite amounts of possibilities. It all depends on the movie. For me, and I consider this very important, I consider the spotting of the movie more important than the composing, because the spotting brings out the concept of what you are going to do in that picture. It is very difficult for me to answer this question in the cold. I must have a subject and give an example.

For instance, suppose you have a car falling from a cliff into the sea. You could start when the car starts to fall, and play the car falling until it hits the sea—the other possibility is that you don't do anything until the moment of the splash of the car into the sea—so all of these things must be discussed with the director of the picture, and if possible, the sound effects man should be in on these conversations so you can discuss where music will go out for sound, and where music will take over in place of sound."

ANSWER FROM MR. FRIEDHOFER

Quote:

"I could give you a very flip answer and say that I determine it emotionally, which is not as flip as it sounds. But actually, in addition to a certain feel that is acquired only through experience, and I hate to ram that down anybody's throat who hasn't been in the business at least a third as long as I have, I should say that you've got to find a way of getting in so that, A, you either make a very strong dramatic point with your entrance, or else, B, you, to use Aaron Copeland's phrase, you sneak the music in as a sort of cushion—a preparatory springboard for something that is going to happen musically of some significance later on. You might not want to start cold on a certain dramatic cue—you might want to lead up to it, but gently."

QUESTION #2. *How do you determine where music shall start and stop in your film?*

ANSWER FROM MR. JONES

Quote:

"My theory is that I try to imagine the various ways that I could play a scene in question. Even if it's open and without dialogue, sometimes silence or sound effects are plenty. I try to imagine what I would play in the scene if I am going to play it. If I run into too many stone walls then maybe it shouldn't be played at all. This is a loaded question because you get into situations where some directors insist on playing love scenes completely with source music. If those were scoring cues, you would have to play them in a completely different way."

ANSWER FROM MR. GOLDSMITH

Quote:

"A good question. Purely emotionally. I have no set formula for it and I can't even give you any logic for it. I see the picture as many times as necessary until I have some kind of emotional response and then I do what my feelings tell me. I have been asked this question so many times and I can only come to the same answer over and over again.

It is something that I feel.

There have been many times where I have spotted the music and where I said there should be music or I was forced to put in music by the director, and it came to the time of writing it and I could not write it. I would put it aside to another day, another day, another day and I could never come up with anything, and I would finally conclude that there should not be music there and I would not write it.

As I said before, I think that it is purely an emotional response."

QUESTION #3. *What special treatment, if any, do you make for playing music under dialogue?*

ANSWER FROM MR. NEWMAN

Quote:

"In my judgement, many composers take the course of least resistance by writing music to be played and recorded at high levels and relying on the dubbing engineer to reduce the level under dialogue.

I think this technique is self-defeating and not nearly as practical as writing (and orchestrating) specifically to accommodate the dialogue.

A useful device is a subtle, gradual diminuendo several bars before the dialogue enters. At this point, the composer is in a position to manipulate his orchestral forces to conform to the dialogue level. He may decide to use solo woodwinds or strings with light accompaniment, or tutti strings, muted, played at levels which would not cloud the dialogue.

I am not implying that the music need be bland. It can be impassioned or romantic, tragic or lyric. I am suggesting that the nuances conform in proper perspective to the dialogue, which in a manner of speaking, is the soloist.

I have strong feelings also about too much motion and elaborate counterpoint under dialogue. It seems to me that dialogue furnishes rhythm, thus a minimum of orchestral motion is desirable. I think dialogue contributes its own counterpoint, hence the danger of complex contrapuntal usage in the accompanying musical score.

Summarizing, I would say that sophisticated simplicity is in order and that light orchestral textures under dialogue are much more effective than clamorous sounds played at low level."

ANSWER FROM MR. SCHIFRIN

Quote:

"Well, first of all, it depends what the dialogue is about. If it is very dramatic and somber and ominous, I have, of course, ominous music. While it may be somber, I try to be very light with the instruments. I try to apply the Opera technique in which when somebody is singing, we go with lesser instrumentation in the orchestra in order not to cover. I want to make my own diminuendo and piano and not rely on sound engineers. I think this is a mission of the composer and he would be wrong to have loud music under dialogue. I think you can say the same thing by making the orchestration lighter."

QUESTION #3. *What special treatment, if any, do you make for playing music under dialogue?*

ANSWER FROM MR. FRIEDHOFER

Quote:

"I think that the mistake that a great many composers, both inexperienced and highly experienced, make, is that they overwrite under dialogue. Either that, or they will duplicate with the rhythmic structure of the music they write under dialogue, the tempo or emotional tension with which the dialogue is spoken. The trick, I think, is to treat dialogue as one or two of three contrapuntal voices that actually are part of your orchestral texture. They become part of the music as I see it."

ANSWER FROM MR. JONES

Quote:

"Maybe some day we will come to an understanding of what areas the voice range plays in. Some voices have low range or low register; even womens voices are not as high as you think and is not that much difference between them and some men. I feel that there are some areas where you can write out of their strata, if you have to, if it's rapid fire dialogue. And if it is nonsensical kind of dialogue, there are many cases where you don't have to be as cautious as if it is plot exposition."

ANSWER FROM MR. GOLDSMITH

Quote:

"Naturally I'm not going to write full brass or wild percussion under dialogue. I think that the timbre of the voice—the placement of the voice range of the actors is extremely important. If you have characters speaking in the middle range, you're not going to write in the middle range. You must stay out of their tonal range with the orchestra. One must keep music as simple as possible, but while it may sound contradictory, there are times when a certain emotional involvement of the music helps too.

I like to use strings and woodwinds—in many cases I'll use nothing but strings or a solo woodwind and strings under dialogue. I like to make it as sustained as possible and as simple as possible, which means that I necessarily must write football notes all the way through it. But I don't like to get too complicated contrapuntally or rhythmically underneath dialogue. If it is a very melodic treatment of a theme, I might try to do it in the simplest, cleanest way.

My own personal feeling is that I think that how I write under dialogue is still based on my own emotional response and I try to keep it as simple as possible."

QUESTION #4. *To what extent does the picture dictate the necessities and style of the music?*

ANSWER FROM MR. NEWMAN

Quote:

"This question seems a bit ambiguous since we are addressing ourselves to music for films—not music per se!

Therefore, I would say, without equivocation that the picture dictates the necessity and style of the musical score, totally.

We are highly involved with world-wide and diverse locales, Biblical subjects, periods in our history, love, sacred and profane, violence, melodrama, the Space Age—comedies and tragedies—to list but a few.

Each situation demands a different approach to a score. Often, exhaustive research is necessary. Jazz and Rock are becoming more and more part of our musical scene.

In any case, the film always must dictate the spirit, style and psychology of any score, however crystalized the composers' personal style may be.

It is in this direction that the composer's versatility is determined.

The film composer must be a man who wears many hats."

ANSWER FROM MR. SCHIFRIN

Quote:

"Well, I think that the picture doesn't dictate the style—it is the style. That means that it is up to the composer to discover the sound of that particular picture and when I say the sound, there are many things implied. For instance, it might be a picture with a locale. It might happen in the Middle East, or Africa, and you would want to bring some Ethnic element into the music. It can be a picture that is absolutely dramatic which is more universal and doesn't apply to Ethnic treatment, but still—there must be a sound that is peculiar to that picture; that is unique and that makes that picture. We must consider that the picture is what it is and not something else and the music must be for that picture and not for any other. Also, the picture might be more abstract. I think that with Documentaries we can be a little more objective, but still, we can bring elements into it that are unique, and make a contribution to the picture. As I said before, it must be an audio-visual counterpoint to the pictorial and dramatic elements in the picture.

"One of the difficult assignments that I had was "The Making Of A President, 1964." I don't want to go into politics here because my problems were as the composer of the film. I had to treat the campaigns of Johnson and Barry Goldwater. The approach was very, very difficult because you have two men—one who has his way of thinking about trying to solve the problems of the country and the other is more conservative in his viewpoints and yet, more controversial. How can you go on these prob-items—well, I solved it by first of all—within the Americana style—by bringing in two definite themes; very different one from the other. The same way that in the fugue you bring in the subject and counter-subject—very different, one from the other. Somtimes, these themes and the overlapping of these themes gave the style of the film. Also for the election day, I planned with the director of the film for a fugue—a real fugue, which showed the American people voting in different sections of the country. And every time there was a map of a new section of the country I would bring in a new element of the fugue. It was a fugue for strings—five voices, because there were five regions of the country. I remember very clearly that it was a strange fugue because each voice had to last for 19 seconds. Towards the end of the election sequence, the fugue becomes really full with all of the voices working one against the other. This is what I mean by trying to solve the particular picture in the style best suited to it.

I could give you other examples, but they would convey that in each picture you have to find the right organic approach. I cannot even decide how I am going to write for a picture by reading the script. A script, for me, is deceiving. I know how to read scores but I don't know how to read scripts. In reading a script, I don't have any feeling of time. You see, film making and music have one thing in common; both happen in time. Words and painting are only in space. You cannot say to me that that painting is about one hour long, but a Symphony is forty minutes long and a film is an hour and a half long. That means that they are both arts that deal in time. Time is the main element here and we have to be very much aware of this and try to solve all of these problems that are happening in time. Scripts are deceiving in time and pace, and these are important considerations in music along with rhythm and flow. I don't get this from reading scripts. Maybe the director or writer gets it because they are used to it, but I don't. I don't even get it by watching the first assembly of a picture. I like to see the final cut and this is what gives me the rhythm, movement, and pace of what the score is going to be."

ANSWER FROM MR. FRIEDHOFER

Quote:

"I will start out with a one word answer, and that is 'completely'. But it dictates it in ways that are again capable of reacting differently on a half a dozen composers, all of whom can be absolutely right in their approach. Personally I am influenced by that ugly little word known as 'mood'—and by mood, I mean actually lighting, camera angles, the pace in which the picture moves, the overall feel of the picture. What is more important is that you try to say with music the things that cannot be said either visually or with dialogue. You try to give the inner meaning of the whole deal. A guy can make love to a gal on the screen, let's say, whose guts he hates, and to play it as a shmaltzy love scene would be wrong. You've got to, if you can get away with it, and the producer will stand for it, try to depict the murder in his heart."

QUESTION #4. *To what extent does the picture dictate the necessities and style of the music?*

ANSWER FROM MR. JONES

Quote:

"It all depends upon the quality of the picture. If an actor has style, or if the particular situation seems to have direction, I really try to be chameleon like with instincts and 'first time down' things that happen to you. You can get motivated with a statue in a room that has nothing to do with the people there that you can play off of, and I try to capture as many visual images to musically help tie the thing together. What's the word—onomatopoeia? That suggests things where the shapes and images of things sometimes suggests a direction. An overall look that the majority of the film covers can sometimes suggest things to you. Again you get into the areas of personalities of people and what things mean to them. I'm a people watcher and I like to transform feelings into musical statements. To me it is like a country; this is completely unrelated, but in a country like Brazil, or Spain, or Portugal, the dance—the seasonings of their food—the speech patterns—the climate—the fruits— everything around the people seems to grow out of some kind of organic source, and I think that a movie should hit you with that same kind of association of piecing together of different elements. Speech patterns, character, moral standards, etc., have to be considered when you are trying to find a direction. Maybe the composite of all of these things can give you a third animal that will be the right vehicle, or the one that you select to go through the picture."

ANSWER FROM MR. GOLDSMITH

Quote:

"That's a marvelous question because I'm faced with this question right now in a picture I am doing. One of my favorite discussions is jumping on the ethnic approach. The ethnic-Oriental is particularly worth talking about because if one were to give the pure ethnological answer musically, they would throw it out in a second. What is ethnic is what Hollywood has made ethnic. Why really, when we do a film that is placed in Mexico, or Italy, or Spain, or—not Germany, because it's hard to play beer hall music under love scenes—or the Orient—anyplace that has a certain poignant or exotic ethnological implication musically, why must we do that? I still say that the majority of films that we work on are made in the United States of America and we don't score them ethnologically, unless we are doing a western. Pure ethnic treatment is a place to hang your hat.

"If we see a picture shot in China, we immediately have the fourths and gongs going. Which was a rather pleasant thing when I did the *Sand Pebbles*, because Bob Wise said, "Don't make it sound like Fu Manchu." Here was a very interesting problem for me. I was playing a very American situation. Here you have the American Navy and you have a real 'book' sailor there, the Captain, who lived by all of the pure Navy traditions—and this is set in a Chinese background, and you have a relationship between an American boy and an American girl, and you have the relationship between a guy called "Frenchy," who is played by an Englishman, who has an affair with a Chinese girl, and you have all of this going on in China on the Yangtse River, supposedly. What a bunch of styles you can get yourself involved in there—and somehow the trick was to make it all compatible—was to have a sort of Oriental wash over it all and yet have it sound very American too. Here I get back to the point of technique. How does one do this? First of all, I started with a very simple basic piece of material. A six note motive which I developed into a love theme. With a couple of little notes here and there, it developed a certain Oriental quality about it. An indication of it. Then it was just a matter of development throughout the picture. Then there was another piece of material that was purely Chinese, but none of it was really that pure Chinese with the fourths and the gongs and all that. It was really a sort of amalgamation of styles. I guess if you ask, "how does the picture dictate this?" it dictated this because I had to have an American situation and an Oriental situation and rather than to say now we are going to play the American, and now we are going to play the Chinese, I wanted to play them all together at once. The characters were there and they were always in the same locale so why should the music jump in locale? I had to have one compatible sound, even through there had to be different thematic ideas.

Now another interesting problem was *The Planet Of The Apes*, which was definitely a science-fiction picture. Now what style does this dictate? I battled this for quite a while. Fortunately, I was assigned to this picture six months before they shot it, so I had nine months to think about it. Not that it did me any good, because until I see the film I really don't know what I am going to do. The obvious—the electronics and all of those gags were the quickest things to forget. What I did on this one was I almost made it a challenge. Sometimes when I am stuck as to what I am going to do, I present myself an imaginary problem and try and solve it. In this situation, I said to myself, 'this picture is so far out and so absurd in many respects, let me do the music in rather an old fashioned way. I will use an old fashioned orchestra with strings, woodwind, and percussion. Unamplified . . . and I'll write a pure twelve-tone score for it . . . and I will not rely on any electronics or on any unusual, per se, type of instrumentation. I will do it purely by music. I will write a very avant-garde, although twelve-tone music is not avant-garde anymore, it's sort of old hat, but for films it is still sort of new . And that is how I did that picture. I guess I'm going to eventually answer this question the same way that I've answered the last two questions. It's what my emotions tell me to do. I can theorize and verbalize, but eventually when it comes to putting down the notes on paper, what I feel inside of me is what's going to come out on paper."

A SUMMARY OF THE SYMPOSIUM

For the author, this experiment was interesting and most gratifying. The interviews were held after the book was written to provide an introduction to the section of this book dealing with the psychology behind composing for films.

All of the composers interviewed are highly respected and their long list of credits speak for themselves.

Each of them is different in viewpoint, in experience, and in his particular approach to music for films.

In this question and answer session, each of them has expressed himself with a viewpoint to technique and philosophy. Each has said what he tries to find in a picture that will stimulate his creative processes. While each of them has a totally different personality guiding his viewpoint, there are many points upon which they all agree.

The principal motivation for what they do is emotional. Can emotional expression be taught? The answer, of course, is no. You as an individual are your own emotional entity. While it is easy to read the emotional processes that these composers have discussed, the best that can be passed on to the novitiate is that the evolution of any kind of music is based on the emotional concept of each individual composer.

What then of these processes can be taught? How does one learn to evaluate and express himself? Is there a way that the emotional values can be learned? In this case, the answer is yes.

It can be taught by procedure. Procedure cannot give you an emotional capacity, but it can sharpen what you already have. It can and will force you to do some serious soul searching, and in the process you may find emotional values in yourself that you did not know existed.

A SYMPOSIUM ON THE COMPOSER'S VIEW TOWARDS
THE PSYCHOLOGY

THE PSYCHOLOGY

Since the time that men began to beat on rocks with sticks, exhorting themselves to do battle with their neighbors, music has played a major part in the structure of our society. In our world of today, we are surrounded by selected and deliberate psychological musical stimulus. Before your inter-continental jet airplane takes off, the cabin of the airplane is flooded with soft, soothing music—designed to lessen the tension; the high speed elevator carries a soft musical background; college bands whip the spectators into a frenzy at sports contests and high class restaurants subscribe to background music designed to give their clients a tasteful and pleasant atmosphere. Companies exist that design and create musical tapes for industrial use. If it is the purpose of the buyer to lessen the tension in a factory dealing with critical components, a program designed to palliate the atmosphere is beamed to the workers throughout the day; if the purpose is to stimulate the output, a program will be specifically set up for that end. The people who construct these background tapes are highly skilled psychologists who know exactly what stimulus is needed and how to select and construct effective programs.

The selected, deliberate, psychological usage of music is the principal burden of the picture composer. This is what film music is about. This is its purpose. The stakes are emotional; the execution selective.

In the hands of the skilled composer, every emotional value will be wrung dry and the audience will receive a heightened impact of the visual and emotional values of the film. Like the skilled psychologist, the skilled composer must be selective in the area of deliberate and calculated psychological stimuli. If he leans on the wrong emotional values, he can warp the picture out of shape.

While it seems impossible to construct a foolproof method of psychological approach to film writing, there do exist procedures that can be used as checkpoints in the designing of a logical sequence of self-imposed questions that can lead to a fuller understanding of the film, its strengths and weaknesses, its benefits and necessities, and the direction in which the composer must go in order to fulfill his obligation and contribution to the film.

THE PSYCHOLOGY OF CREATING MUSIC
FOR FILMS

CHAPTER 1

THE APPROACH

Each composer must ask of himself many pertinent questions in the discharge of his responsibilities.

I have always given my pupils the following words and asked them to arrange them in the order of their own musical importance:

WHAT?   * * * What kind of music shall I write?

WHO?   * * * Who will play the music I write?

WHY?   * * * Why should there be music in the scene?

WHEN?   * * * When should music start and when should it finish?

WHERE? * * * Where does the music belong in the scene?

The arrangement of these words indicate an approach to an applied psychology. There are no rules for psychology in music. It can and must be as flexible as the film itself. The problems of a documentary with (or without) narration are vastly different than the problems of a cartoon. The problems of a musical are not the same as those of a situation comedy. Still, there must be at least a procedure in thinking.

THE APPROACH

The composer must train himself to be aware of the problems of the film with which he is associated. He must know the film inside out and backwards. He must understand what the people before him have tried to say. If he is not sure of the intent of a scene or group of scenes, he must go to the people who have preceeded him aesthetically and discuss their viewpoints. He has an obligation to carry out their intentions as well as those of his own.

Before he can break his film down into scenes which must be covered by music, he must thoroughly understand the strengths and weaknesses of the film.

Finally, he must learn to trust his picture. The one factor in his performance as a composer that remains immutable is the picture itself. If he knows his picture, what it is about, where it has succeeded and where it has failed, then- and only then-is he in a position to exercise creative judgment. In all cases, the picture comes first. The composer who writes music for the sake of music itself, and ignores his picture, has a pretty good chance of becoming eminently unsuccessful.

The successful composer is the man who can adapt himself to work on the weaknesses of the picture and let the strengths take care of themselves. He must train himself to think in terms of picture values. If he knows his film—if he can develop the ability to think in terms of dramatics and theatrics—if he can develop the control over his medium so that the mechanics work for him and nuances in photographic techniques are matched by subtle specifics in the orchestra—then he is in a position to worry about what kind of music he will write.

Once a composer really knows all there is to know about his film, the notes are easy to find. If he does not know his film, the notes are impossible to find.

CHAPTER 2

WHY?

WHY MUSIC?

The most important question that the composer must ask himself is *WHY?* It is also the most important question he must ask others if a pre-judgement has been made that a scene must be scored. Why? Why *must* there be music? If this sounds negative, remember that there are many things that music can do and many things it cannot. The dramatic stage play exists almost entirely without music and suffers not at all. The light opera and musical comedy forms of theater would be dead without it. Music is the total life blood of that medium. In films, the usage of music is selective.

Music can do many things, but it cannot save a bad scene. This is the most common form of misusage of music in the film industry. Invariably in a projection room at the conclusion of a bad scene you will hear the comment, "That scene is weak, maybe music can save it." Music can't save it. It is possible that music may make the scene more palatable. Music can make a scene more dramatic or less dramatic, but if the audience does not see on the screen what the composer is trying to say, the music will not be successful. Music cannot make an unfunny scene funny. Sometimes, even by a far-out approach, music can burlesque a scene and make it more effective. Sometimes by sharpening the visual accents of a scene, it can make the scene appear more stylized than it really is. Music can also spoil a good dramatic or comedy scene. There are times when what is on the screen represents 100% of the dramatic value that the picture can stand. The addition of music at this point would be to make the scene melodramatic. The solution in this case is to stay out.

It would appear that I am attempting to discourage the use of music entirely. On the contrary, what I am trying to say is that the most frequent failure of music in pictures comes from putting music in the wrong place and for the wrong purpose.

EFFECTIVE MUSIC HEIGHTENS THE EMOTIONAL STAKES.

It's as simple as that! There will be areas where you cannot obviously or visually justify the reason for music in a scene. The sole purpose of it being there is that you feel the necessity of heightening the emotional stakes.

This is the total case for scoring—this is its purpose. Like nutmeg and ginger, a little of it goes a long way. Earlier, the statement was made that the real masters of the art and craft of film music writing were masters of understatement. I believe this to be true. If the answer to WHY?—Why must there be music?—is because it is *dramatically* necessary, then you have qualified your reason for scoring the scene.

There is one rule that you can lean on:

YOU NEVER GO INTO A SCENE UNLESS YOU HAVE SOMETHING TO SAY THAT WILL HELP THE PICTURE EMOTIONALLY!

CHAPTER 3

WHERE?

The second step in the Spotting* procedure is to decide <u>*WHERE*</u> music shall go. This does not have to be a specific decision, yet. It is conceivable that a very long sequence of five minutes or more must be scored in its entirety. It is also conceivable that it might only require scoring in part of the total scene. Recognizing that music has to go into a certain scene is important, but the principal determination is to pinpoint exactly <u>*WHERE*</u> it will register the greatest impact. This can often affect a change of decision as to the actual start and stop of the cue. There will be times when you break down an entire sequence and start to work on it. For some reason, that doesn't clear up right away, it begins to feel wrong. This is brought on by actually working with the scene. You will find that many times you have selected the proper place to put music, but the right place to start and stop escapes you. The more you work with a sequence of this type, the more you will find that you feel the necessity to adjust the start or stop of the cue. As your feeling for the finer values begin to crystallize, you will begin to get down to the specifics of "<u>*WHEN?*</u>".

*See glossary

CHAPTER 4

WHEN?

<u>WHEN</u> do you go in? <u>WHEN</u> do you get out? These determinations are arrived at by a combination of showmanship, instinct, experience and examination. There are times when you decide that the entrance of music, which is almost always felt, should be Sneaked*. This means that the music enters in as unobtrusive a manner as is possible. Usually, you look for a sound effect of some sort to mask the entrance of the music. As the effect dies away, the music is in without being felt too strongly. Perhaps you decide to enter on a dialogue cue. This always produces an effect in direct proportion to the music you write and can be a quiet reflective entrance—or a thunderous one. In these examples, the use of the word perhaps, is necessary. The kind of entrance you use is personal unto you and the kind of music you write, and can be as varied as the situations to which you are exposed. It is for you, the composer, to decide whether an entrance is to be understated, stated, or overstated.

As an illustration, let's use a common device, the gunshot. "Two cowboys face each other on a deserted street. Suddenly, one of them draws and fires. The other is hit and falls heavily to the ground. The cowboy in the white hat walks over to the heavy in the black hat who makes some last profound statement—and dies. The people of the town pour out of the shops onto the street to congratulate the hero who turns scornfully from them, mounts his horse and rides off into the sunset." Where have you seen this before? Well, what about the gunshot? Does the music build up to the gunshot and cut off leaving the shot in the clear and then catch the heavy being hit? Does it enter as he falls? Does it come in as he dies? Does it come in as the hero rides off into the sunset? When? When does it start? If it builds up to a climax and cuts off before the gunshot, the start has to be in somewhere earlier in the cue. <u>WHEN?</u> and <u>WHERE?</u> and <u>WHY?</u> The answer to this particular question, which is the end of our picture, might have been set up by something you did in the first reel. If this is the culmination of our picture, it should not come out of context but should be part of everything you have tried to say from the very beginning of the picture. Whatever creative process you have used from the beginning should be fulfilled in the end. A realization of the creative values you have tried to express in your score will answer the question of what happens with the gunshot. The answer should and must be personal to you and reflect your dramatic opinion.

*See glossary

THE PSYCHOLOGY OF CREATING MUSIC
FOR FILMS

CHAPTER 5

WHAT? — AND WHO?

WHAT kind of music shall I write?

This, in my estimation, is the first time that music, in the sense of composition, comes into consideration. You have now brought all of the mechanical and dramatic values to the point where you can start to consider the music itself. By now you should have a full understanding of the necessities involved and begin to search for notes. What kind of music you write will depend on your own viewpoint about music. As long as the total burden of what you have to do is understood and crystallized, you can go to work with pencil and paper.

WHO will play the music I write?

This is the last step in the psychological process. Who will play what is governed, in some sense, by the size of the orchestra available to you. Cost enters its ugly head and becomes a prime factor in the size of the combination. If you are on a low budget project, you are naturally going to be working with small combinations.

These smaller combinations must be designed very carefully to produce the maximum result of the kind of music you write. Although it is hard to make large effects with small groups, T.V. has proven that small combinations, carefully selected, can and do make some very effective music.

After all, in today's recording medium, with reverberation, equalization (and the like) available, music takes on the aural effect that a puppet show accomplishes visually. In television specifically, smaller groups do not suffer as much as on the large motion picture screen. The smaller combo actually suffers less than larger ones when coming out of a 4-inch speaker.

Although this book is not designed to discuss the problems of music, as such, it seems necessary to remind you that the quickest way of making a small combo sound small is to have everybody playing all of the time. Once the ear has adjusted to everyone playing, it is almost impossible to make a climax of any kind. I refer to smaller combos only because this book is directed at the novice who seldom has the opportunity to start out with fifty men, or more.

CHAPTER 6

DIALOGUE IS COUNTERPOINT

It is. It has line, pace and pitch. It also has emotional values of all kinds. Learn to treat dialogue with respect and make it work for you.

There are two different ways of handling music under dialogue. One technique is to pay little attention to it and depend on reducing the level of the orchestra when the film is dubbed. The other accepts dialogue and uses it as counterpoint.

If you have a large enough orchestra, you can make less accommodation for dialogue. The reason for this is that the large orchestra doesn't lose its body when dubbed to a low level. The small orchestra does.

Today's Hi-Fi pre-amplifiers have a compensation switch built into them. When the level is dropped, this compensating circuit automatically adds the lows and highs that are lost by the drop in level. While the volume may change, the contour of the music does not. In the film business the process of dubbing is manual. Under the always present press of time, it is almost impossible to expect a man to equalize level drops in track without suffering some losses. Where the Hi-Fi circuitry is automatic, the control of the film circuitry is manual. All of the frailties of the personal touch of the music mixer in dubbing are amplified by tracks under dialogue that contain drastic level changes. The safest solution for the dubbing mixer is to play the entire track at so low a level that the music loses design, substance, and effect.

To have effective music under dialogue, you must write it effectively. This is not a case for making music under dialogue completely bland. On the contrary. Successful writing under dialogue demands the most careful attention. There is nothing that prevents you from reducing the size of your combination. You can go from the full tutti of a large orchestra down to small combinations of strings and/or woodwinds. Solo instruments work beautifully behind dialogue as long as you are careful about their projection, register and timbre. If the dialogue climbs in intensity, so can the music. However, to use an extreme example, if the people in the scene are whispering, forget the idea that open brass, or any other heavy effect, won't intrude. It will.

One of the most startling effects in music is sudden silence. A key line left in the open can be intensified unbelievably. By the same token, a kiss on the screen doesn't always need a harp glissando or a surge of Ravel. Going out with the music and playing the moment in silence can be intensely effective. Silence or near silence can work for you if you use your imagination and pick your spots very carefully.

THE PSYCHOLOGY OF CREATING MUSIC
FOR FILMS

We have previously discussed the pace of music under dialogue. It should be reiterated at this point. Learn to expand your music under dialogue. If you need movement, look for unobtrusive patterns. Some of the best picture writers are expert in the usage of vamps. You don't necessarily recognize them as being vamps because they set up slow harmonic or rhythmic patterns that are relatively complete. At the proper moment they add a long line melody to their pattern and get tremendous mileage out of simple means.

Remember that sharp level changes behind dialogue usually do not work. Unless you are punctuating between lines of dialogue for effect, the sharp level changes will intrude. The small orchestra can be as guilty of this intrusion as the large. Train yourself to write for dialogue. Learn to recognize the nuances—the inflections that the people speaking are using, the intent, the emotion and the level of dialogue can be used as counterpoint.

The time to display your musical contrapuntal technique is when the music is uncovered—out in the clear. At this point you can pull out all of the stops and let go with both barrels—as long as it fits the picture.

Examples #35 and #36 show two different types of scoring under dialogue. The first was slow music under dialogue of very personal nature. The second was done to click track to provide the orchestra with an easy pace. Once again, the cue sheets will give you the intent and substance of the scene. The scores will show you how these two different kinds of scenes were handled musically. While both of these scenes worked well, I'm sure that there will be new and different devices for handling dialogue as long as words continue to be written for the screen. While no two scenes may be identical, you can bet that the successful ones, from the scoring standpoint, will have been written by composers who have respect for the words and the technique to accommodate them in the most flattering way.

EXAMPLE #35

I SPY #26   696'

M 24/31-PICTURE

:00   Start on center of Dissolve to baby after K says:
             "AH, YES." K & S exchanging cigars

:00 2/3   Full in dissolve

:03 1/2   Camera pans up to reveal Angela holding baby, smiling

:09   End of reel #2 - beginning Reel #3

:09   Cut - hospital room - K & S entering, S holding flowers-
:14   Camera pans with them as they walk across room

:19   Pan reveals Angela
:20
:20 1/2   S lays flowers on bed next to her

:24   They are looking at baby and S reaches over to touch it.
:25   S: "DAD, THAT IS A BEAUTIFUL BABY YOU'VE GOT THERE."
             (ends :27 1/2)

:28 2/3   K, touching baby: "WHAT ARE YOU GONNA CALL HER?"
:31   (ends :29 1/2)

:32 1/3   Angela: "I'LL HAVE HER READY IN A DAY OR SO FOR THE
             WORLD AND THEN I'LL NAME HER...RIGHT NOW I WANT HER
             UNCLUTTERED ---"

:38 1/3   Cut C.S. Angela: "RIGHT NOW, SHE'S JUST MY BABY"
             (ends :40 2/3)

:40 2/3   Cut - 2 shot K & S

:42 1/3   Cut C.S. Angela

:42 1/2   Angela: "THANK YOU FOR THE FLOWERS."(ends :43 1/2)

:43 1/2   Cut - 2 shot K & S

:45 1/3   S: "YOUR BABY'S GONNA MAKE A DIFFERENCE IN THE WAY
             YOU ---" (ends :47 1/3) S looks up

:47 1/3   Cut Full shot nurse walking into scene

:49 1/3   Nurse, in Spanish to Angela - dialogue.
             Angela: "BRING HER BACK SOON" Nurse answers in Sp.
:50 1/2   (ends :53)

                                             continued...

EXAMPLE #35 (Cont.)

I SPY #26

M-24/31   (page 2)

⊕:54
:58 1/3   Nurse exits with baby as trio watches, S laughing

:58 2/3   Cut - nurse walking out of door

1:00 1/2   Cut - 2 shot K & S

⊕1:01
1:01 1/2   S: "I WAS JUST SAYING THAT YOUR BABY'S GONNA MAKE A
            DIFFERENCE IN THE WAY YOU'VE BEEN THINKING."
            (ends 1:05 1/2)

1:05 1/2   Cut C.S. Angela. She looks down

1:07 2/3   Angela: "SHE HAS...SHE'S MADE UP MY MIND FOR ME."
⊕1:08   (ends 1:09 2/3)

1:09 2/3   Cut - 2 shot K & S

1:10 2/3   S looks to K reacting to her statement.
            K: "HOW?"

1:11 1/2   Cut C.S. Angela: "I CAN'T GO BACK TO THE STATES.. NOT
            EVER." (ends 1:13 1/2)

1:13   Cut - 2 shot K & S

1:13 2/3   K closes eyes
(1:15)
1:16 1/3   K: "WHY NOT?" (ends 1:16 2/3)

1:16 2/3   Cut C.S. Angela: "SHE DOESN'T HAVE A FATHER."
            (ends 1:18 1/3)

1:18 1/3   Cut - 2 shot K & S. K: "OH, HONEY, COME ON - TIMES
            HAVE CHANGED. PEOPLE DON'T POINT THEIR FINGER ANY MORE.
⊕1:22   THEY DON'T EVEN HAVE TO KNOW." (ends 1:25 2/3)

1:24 2/3   Cut - C.S. Angela

1:26   Angela: "WELL, I'D KNOW, EVENTUALLY SHE'D KNOW. PEOPLE
            DO POINT WHERE I LIVE, THEY DO ---"(ends 1:30 1/2)
⊕1:29
1:29 1/3   Cut - 2 shot K & S

continued....

EXAMPLE #35 (Cont.)   179

I SPY #26

M-24/31 (page 3)

1:31 1/2	Cut C.S. Angela: "--- HERE IN MEXICAO ALL THEY'D SAY IS SHE'S BEAUTIFUL --- I'M STAYING HERE." (ends, 1:36½)
⊕1:36	
1:36 1/2	Cut - 2 shot K & S
1:37	K: "ANGEL, YOU'RE HELPLESS HERE --- THE WORD IS OUT TIBA IS AFTER YOU. HE'S BEEN A STEP BEHIND YOU SINCE STOCKHOLM." (ends 1:42 2/3)
1:39½	
1:40 2/3	Cut C.S. Angela
1:42 2/3	Angela: "TIBA HAS NOT TAKEN OVER MEXICO ✱ WHOEVER TIBA IS' (ends 1:45 2/3)
⊕1:44½	
1:45 2/3	2 shot K & S
1:46 1/3	K: "MISS MARCH, YOU ARE AN AGENT WITH THE KIND OF JOB YOU CANNOT WALK AWAY FROM. AT LEAST NOT UNTIL YOU WALK HOME." (ends 1:51 2/3)
⊕1:49½	
1:51 2/3	Cut C.S. Angela xx shaking her head
1:52 2/3	Angela: "PLEASE GO AWAY." (ends 1:54)
1:54 1/3	Full shot. S: "IF TIBA CATCHES UP TO YOU WHAT HAPPENS TO THE BABY THEN?" (ends 1:56 2/3)
⊕1:56⅓	
1:56 2/3	Angela: "I CAN'T DO IT. I CAN'T GO BACK!"(ENDS 1:58 2/3'
1:59 2/3	Cut - shot of nurse walking thru door. Nurse goes into Spanish dialogue. (ends 2:02 1/3)
2:02 1/3	Cut - full shot K, S & Angela
2:03	K turns to S
2:04 2/3	S to K: "VISITING HOURS ARE OVER." K: "ALRIGHT -- LISTEN, VISITING HOURS ARE TWICE A DAY, AND WE'LL BE HERE LIKE CLOCKWORK. YOU CAN COUNT ON IT" (ends 2:12 2/3)
⊕2:06	
2:12 2/3	
2:14 1/2	K reaches over and kisses Angela on forehead. K: "YOU'RE GOING BACK. YOU HAVE TO." (ends 2:17 1/3 as he raises up, smiling)

EXAMPLE #35 (Cont.)

I SPY # 26

M-24/31 (page 4)

2:18	They start out - camera panning with them
2:21 1/2	They pass nurse at door and acknowledge goodbyes
2:25 1/3	Nurse, staying in room, closes door and she walks over to Angela - camera panning with her
2:30	Nurse, smiling at Angela, picks up bouquet
2:33	Angela, concerned and weary, pulls covers up around her neck
2:35 1/3	Start Fade out
2:36 1/3	Full out
2:36 1/3	Start Fade in on S hand reaching in bouquet for ~~xxxx~~ flower.
2:37 2/3	Full in
2:39	S's hand goes off scene as camera pans up to him
2:39 2/3	S: "HERE."

(END MUSIC IN FADE OUT)

TOTAL TIME   2:36 1/3

EXAMPLE #35 A

EXAMPLE #35A (Cont.)

EXAMPLE #35 A (Cont.)

EXAMPLE #35A (Cont.)

EXAMPLE #36

I SPY #43   Stut 479'

M-14

9 FRAME Cut
9 WARN

Tonia, quite hostile in general attitude,
has been confronted by Scott who is trying to
'break-the-ice' with a few reasonable questions.
He finally introduces himself as Alexander Scott,
and she has said: " I'M TONIA. " They shake hands
and she moves O.S. saying as she gestures:
" MI SEQUE. " (Follow Me.)

:00   Music Starts just after Tonia's line. She is
            O.S. and Scott remains seated in a street doorway.

:01   Scott begins move to get up to follow her -
            still puzzled but yet intrigued by her.

:02 1/3   Scott trots out of scene @ L to pursue Tonia.

:02 2/3   Cut to a rather squalid looking yard with kids
            playing with cardboard boxes. The camera follows
            their play, panning R.

:06 1/3   O.S. we hear Tonia'svvoice starting out with
            her 'life story' as camera brings in a small
            boy seated by a trash can: " I WAS SIX YEARS
            OLD WHEN I CAME TO THIS COUNTRY. "(Ends :08 2/3)

:08   The boy hears them and peeks out from a
            protecting piece of cardboard.

:08 2/3   Cut to Full Shot of Scott walking alongside
            Tonia-approaching camera. Camera follows them L-R.

:09 1/3   Tonia continues: " MY MOTHER WAS A U.S.O. PERFORM-
            ER - AN AMERICAN, SHE LIKED IT HERE AND SHE
            STAYED. HOW DO YOU LIKE MY START, MR. SCOTT? "

:16 2/3   Scott replies: " WELL, IT'S , AH, ASIDE FROM THE
            FACT THAT IT'S ITALY IT'S NO DIFFERENT FROM MY
            OLD NEIGHBORHOOD - I'VE RODE CARDBOARD BOXEX
            'N EVERYTHING ---- "

Ex:23 1/3   Tonia breaks in: " YA KNOW, I HAPPEN TO KNOW
            THAT AMERICANS THINK THAT POOR PEOPLE ARE MOR-
            ALLY INFERIOR. " Scott: " AHH! " Tonia continues:
            " I KNOW THIS BECAUSE MY MOTHER TAUGHT ME. SHE
            TAUGHT ME HOW TO SPEAK YOUR LANGUAGE, BUT SHE
            TAUGHT ME NOT TO THINK YOUR THOUGHTS. "

:35   Scott: " I SEE, SO WHAT KIND OF THOUGHTS DO
            YOU THINK NOW? "

:38 1/3   Tonia answers: " I THINK THAT I AM AS GOOD
            AS ANYONE. "

:40 2/3   Scott: " YES---- "

:41 2/3   Tonia: " THAT I AM FREE---- "

:42   Scott: " RIGHT---- "

:42 1/2   Tonia: " THAT I AM NOT SOMEONE'S SERVANT! "

                                        (cont'd.)

EXAMPLE #36 (Cont.)

I SPY #43

M-14 (P. 2.)

:44 2/3   Scott: " LISTEN, I GIVE YA THAT - I AGREE. "

:46 2/3   Tonia: " DID YOU SEE ME EARLIER TODAY OUTSIDE
           THE TENNIS CLUB SELLING PASTRIES? " (Ends :50)

:51 1/3   Scott: " YOU MEAN THAT LITTLE CART? THAT WAS
           YOU? " She nods. Scott continues: " I ALMOST
           RAN OVER AND BOUGHT PASTRIES. "

:55 1/3   Tonia - as though proving her point: " BUT YOU
           WERE MUCH TOO BUSY CARRYING THE WHITE MAN'S
           RACQUETS! " (Ends :58 1/3)

:59 2/3   Scott - a little stumped about replying: " OH
           NOW YOU'RE WRONG, LADY,BECAUSE THAT'S NOT MY---- "

1:02 ½   Tonia breaks in: " AH I MAY LOOK STUPIDO TO YOU,
           MR. SCOTT, BUT I HAPPEN TO KNOW WHAT CONDITIONS
           ARE IN YOUR COUNTRY. "

1:08 2/3   Scott: " OH NOW - WHAT KIND OF CONDITIONS HAVE WE?"

1:11 1/3   Tonia: " RUTHLESS EXPLOITATION OF RACIAL MINORITIES

1:14 1/3   Scott: " I SEE,---AND CAPITALIST WAR MONGERS,
           AND THEIR WALL STREET LACKYS, AND ALSO WHERE
           THE RICH FOLK LIVE---- "

1:20 1/3   Tonia breaks in: " MR. SCOTT, I DON'T WANT TO
           TALK ABOUT IT ANYMORE! I SUGGEST THAT YOU GO
           HOME, AND AH, YOUR MASTER WILL BE ANGRY !"(end
                                                  1:27 1/3)

234 1:27 1/3   Tonia starts walking rapidly away as camera
                pans her away.

1:31 ½   Start Dissolve.

250 1:33 ½   We hear Kelly's O.S. voice as door clicks to
              open and K. & S. enter: " ALL RIGHT! ALREADY -
              LET'S SEE! LISTEN!

                            TOTAL TIME   1:33 ½

EXAMPLE #36   Record Band #15

EXAMPLE #36   (Cont.)

EXAMPLE #36   (Cont.)

CHAPTER 7

THE DIFFERENT TYPES OF SCORING

There are three basic types of scoring.

1. Qualified or implied source.

2. Source scoring.

3. Pure scoring.

The selection of which of these to use and when to use them is a principal decision on the part of the composer. A thorough understanding of the motivation for these different techniques is of vital importance to the composer.

The ability to select the right one at the right time not only keeps the composer from trapping himself in an awkward medium, but may even give him a style that can serve him throughout the whole picture.

It is possible that a whole picture may involve only one of these basic techniques. It is equally possible that a picture score may use all three as well as a mixture of more than one at a time.

Technique #1 — SOURCE MUSIC

Source music applies to a <u>visual</u> <u>source</u> or an <u>implied</u> <u>source</u>. The example of the people dancing is scored with source music—whether the source of the music, a band, a juke box, a radio, or whatever, is visual or not. If the source of the music is visual, the usage is obligatory. If the source is visual and involves the actions of live musicians, then the usage of source is not only obligatory but the movements should be matched. See Example #37. In the case of the source not being visual, the usage of source music is selective. Source music is usually popular in style. It can cover the field of popular music from rock-and-roll to show tunes. It must always be in character to the scene it covers in particular and the picture as a whole. If a picture is of a particular era, say the 1920's, the source would naturally be of that era and in the character of the times.

In the earlier days of the motion picture business, elaborate devices were used to qualify source music. A scene would start on a close up of a record spinning and pull back and pan to two people sitting on a sofa playing a love scene. This was the directors way of saying that he wanted this scene played in a popular style. What he was really doing was qualifying the source of the music.

EXAMPLE #37

With the advent of composers such as Henry Mancini, source and implied source have been accepted as a solid style of music to score with whether the source is qualified or not. We refer to Qualified Source as any situation that does, or could have, a legitimate source. If we use a cocktail piano cue in a bar-room scene, it makes no difference whether you see the pianist or not. The fact that the character of the music is indigenous to the setting of the scene, qualifies it. If we use juke box music behind a scene in an ice cream parlor, it is qualified whether we see the juke box or not. The fact that it is a logical kind of music to use makes it right. In this case, the usage of that type of source music becomes selective. You use it because you want to; not because you are obliged to. Source and Qualified source are the most important kinds of music to use in certain kinds of scenes. It would be far better to use source to cover a scene between two teenagers sitting in a car at a drive-in, than to attempt the dramatic license of out-and-out scoring. In these cases, the source approach is more in character with the scene and with the people.

The usage of Ethnic Source in foreign locale is invaluable in establishing character and location. The mandolins of Italy, the guitars of Spain, the bagpipes of Scotland can do miracles in setting the stage geographically. In period pictures, even the scoring takes on the character of the source music of the times.

Source music generally states its premise in an overall way. This is to say that the character of the whole piece of music is used to score the intent of a scene. If the nature of the scene is frenetic, the pace and drive of the music can be used to underline the intent of the scene. While you may wish to catch specific points of action in a scene using source music, it is always sound to let the whole piece make an overall effect and catch your self-designated changes of action with natural devices in the music. The fewer picture cues you catch with source, the better.

The usage of pace and character in source music is vital. It may suit your dramatic purpose to play against the character of a scene. Source music handles this kind of situation admirably. It succeeds in many instances where scoring fails, because of its overall nature. Large blocks of film can be covered by source music of one kind or another.

TRANSITIONS IN SOURCE

The transition from source to scoring and vice versa can accomplish enormous changes in character, location, and time between two scenes. If we wish the transition from scoring to source or source to scoring, to be smooth and practically unnoticeable, we use key relationships and key matching carefully and make our overlaps to specific points in the music. If we want to feel the change in character, we deliberately make our key relationships unrelated and allow the two tracks to grind harmonically for the moment of crossover to feel the entrance of the new track.

"BLOCKING OUT" A SOURCE SCENE

In laying out a source music scene, there are several considerations we must make. Let us assume that the scene we are going to cover is quite long and requires more than one piece of music to cover its length.

The first consideration we must make is, "should the character of the music change from one piece of music to another, and if so, where?" Our first operation is to "block out" the scene. The practical way to do this if there is no visual obligation to match, such as dancing, is to get an overall dialogue timing of the whole scene. (Example #38). By carefully studying the dialogue timing, we can pick the places to start and stop the music. If we are in a night club, for example, we can assume five or six seconds between numbers. If we wish to give the effect that the music is "going" when we enter the scene, we must lay it out that way. We generally lay this out to read — <u>Make overlong in front and back in</u> to the specific spot at which we wish the music to stop. If the music is to be heard "going" as it comes in, it must of necessity have some extra bars in front, two or four bars is enough, to get the band started and actually be "going" at :00 of the cue. The completed track is dialed in at :00 and really is "going" when you first hear it. If we are going into a scene on a direct cue, we still make the track overlong, back it in to the stop point, and cut the front part of the track off to match the picture cut. The bars of music that we add in front of the actual start of any cue are designated as "A" and "B" bars, or "A," "B" and "C" and "D". These letters indicate that these bars are added for the purpose of getting the orchestra started.

At the end of a scene, if we wish to give the impression that the activity is still going on, we use a track that is overlong at the end and either dial it out in the dissolve, or cut it off at the cut. If we wish a track to put a period on the finish of a scene, we use either a natural start to natural finish or an overlong start to a natural finish, depending on the length of the cue. These are the four basic types of source music designations:

1. Overlong in front to a natural finish.

2. Overlong in front and back.

3. Natural start to a natural finish.

4. Natural start to an overlong finish.

If there are no visual obligations to be met, these source music cues can be done wild to stop watch or clicks and placed where we wish. Overlong tracks, front or rear, can be made to any length longer than the minimum requirements as long as there are no visual obligations to be met. If there are, we have to go to the bar breakdown technique in order to get our picture match.

It is impossible to list the many ways that source music can work for you. By all means, develop the facility to use it freely. No other technique can cover large blocks of film so easily and say so much with so little effort.

BLOCKING OUT A SOURCE MUSIC SCENE FROM CUE SHEETS
(See Example #38)

There is no necessity to reproduce the actual music used in this scene. The principle problem is to create a background atmosphere and the cue sheet layout tells how it was done.

After an on-stage vocal number by "Lori," the star of a Las Vegas nightclub, the scene dissolved to her dressing room and a dramatic scene was played. To keep the background atmosphere alive, the logical choice was that of a small combo ostensibly coming from a between-show lounge. Inasmuch as the scene started on a dissolve from the end of her number on-stage to Lori in her dressing room off-stage, the dissolve indicated a passage of time and a change of location. The small combo piece was made "Wild" to be more than 1:34 in length. The track was backed in to end at one thirty-four (1:34) and allowed to run overlong at the beginning of the dissolve. This piece of music was made without clicks and routined to last about 1:50, to a finish. By backing the track in to end at 1:34 the dial-on at :00 gave the effect that the combo had been playing for an undetermined length of time before the scene started. The time lapse between 1:34 and 1:38 and 2/3rds was filled in with applause. At 1:38 and 2/3rds, the combo started into a piece of material—"Lori"—which was the theme of the show. This was done in the most simple fashion using just rhythm and a tenor sax solo. This piece was recorded in a very slow tempo (21-4clx) and covered the rest of the scene from 1:38 and 2/3rds to 4:57 where she starts to make a phone call. The applause for the end of this number trailed out as her conversation started and ended just before we cut away to the person to whom she was talking on the phone.

All of the off-stage music was dubbed in an off-stage perspective. The simplicity of an implied source combo playing a very plaintive melody against a highly dramatic scene is one of the most effective devices we have. This kind of background matches the scene being played in the most overall kind of way. It reflects only the character of a principal in the picture and allows the dramatics to find high points and low points without being matched by the music. In a peculiar way, the scene gains intensity because as it builds, it overpowers the back ground and as it relaxes the background is once again felt. I cannot recommend too strongly the judicious useage of source or implied source to play with or against dramatic scenes. It can, of course, be tailored to rise and fall with the scene, but as a rule, the overall effect is better when it is not too detailed.

EXAMPLE #38

"I SPY" # 30

M-33, Off stage source, picture?   367

"another Min Blues"

Min. 54 Bars.

To END at 1:34 overlay in Frt.

.00	After Lorrie has finished second number - start on beginning of dissolve... to Lorrie in dressing.
.02	Full in - there is knocking at the door.
.02 2/3	Lorrie:"COME IN."
.06 2/3	Scotty:(as he ~~enters~~ enters):"HEY."
.08 1/3	He stops in background and she sees him in ~~the~~ mirror.
.08 2/3	Lorrie, getting up and going over to him:"SCOTTY!"
.09 1/3	Scotty: "HEY , HOW ARE YOU DOING?"
.10 1/2	She runs over to him.
.11 1/2	They embrace and ad lib greetings
.13 2/3	Lorrie: "HOW ARE YOU?"
.14 2/3	Scotty: "I'M ALL RIGHT."
	They continue adlibbing, etc.
.19 2/3	Scotty: "SAY HELLO TO KELLY ROBINSON."
.22	Lorrie, stepping over to Kelly:"WELL HI KEL - HOW ARE YOU? ANY FRIEND OF SCOTTY'S - HAS GOT TO BE A FRIEND OF MINE. COME ON, MAKE YOURSELF A DRINK."
.28 1/3	They step across the dressing room.
.31	Kelly:"CAN I MAKE ONE FOR YOU?"
.32 2/3	Lorrie: "OH NO - I NEVER TOUCH IT ANYMORE."
.37	Kelly begins preparing his drink.
.37 1/2	Lorrie: "NOT ANYMORE."
.38 1/3	Kelly: " IS THAT RIGHT? WELL MY MAN HERE IS THE SAME WAY. ONE OF THE GREAT PURISTS OF ALL TIMES. SOME TIMES I FEEL LIKE I'M UP TO MY HEAD IN MISSIONARYS OR SOMETHING."
48 1/2	He raises his glass towards Lorrie and says "TO BEAUTY."

Continued

EXAMPLE #38 (Cont.)

"I SPY" # 30

M-33(Continued, Page 2)

49 2/3	He looks over to Scotty.
50 1/2	Kelly:" ... AND THE BEAST."
.55	Lorrie: "HEY SCOTTY, HOW'S THE SPY BUSINESS."
.57 2/3	Kelly:"WHAT DID YOU SAY?"
1.00	Lorrie: "I SAID HOW'S THE SPY BUSINESS?"
1.03 1/2	Kelly to Scotty: "WHAT'S SHE TALKING ABOUT?"
1.04 1/3	Lorrie: "GET YOU TWO, I LOVE YOUR ACT - ALL YOU HAVE TO DO IS COREOGRAPH IT AND I'LL BET YOU I CAN GET YOU BOOKED."
1.14	Scotty: " I RECRUITED HER BROTHER, REMEMBER?"
1.18 1/3	Lorrie starts over to Scotty.
1.19 1/3	They ad lib how good it is to see each other.
1.20 2/3	They embrace and continue ad libbing.
1.24 1/2	Scotty: "LISTEN, YOU KNOW WHAT WE HAVE TO DO? WE HAVE TO GO OUT AND DELEBRATE, RIGHT NOW. WHAT YOU DO IS YOU CALL ▆ JIM AND WE'LL GO OUT ON THE TOWN."
1:34	Lorrie: "JIM?"
1.34 1/2	
1.35 13/	Scotty: "YES --"
1.35 2/3	Cut, close shot, Kelly, watching.
	Scotty(continued, offstage) " ... COME ON, JIM."
1.38	Cut medium full shot, Scott, ▆▆▆▆ Lorrie and Kelly in foregroudn.
1.38 2/3	Lorrie starts to step away from Scotty.
1.42 1/2	Lorrie, stopping by dressing table" YOU DON'T KNOW- ▆ YOU REALLY DON'T KNOW?"
1.46	Scotty:"NO"
1.51 1/3	Lorrie:"JIM'S DEAD"

Finish M.33

APPLAUSE

Start M33A
"LORI"

21-6

(Continued)

EXAMPLE #38 (Cont.)

"I SPY" # 30

M-33 (continued, page 3)

W33A

1.52 1/3		Cut, close shot, Kelly as he reacts slightly.
1.54 1/2		Cut, medium two shot, Lorrie and Scotty.
1.55		Lorrie: "HE, HE -- DROWNED -- HE WAS SCUBA DIVING OFF OF CATALINA ISLAND AND HE NEVER CAME UP."
2.07		She sits down at dressing table.
2.08 2/3		Lorrie(continued) "THEY NEVER --THEY NEVER ▮▮▮ FOUND HIM. OH THEY GAVE HIM A FEW LINES ON A RADIO STATION-THAT WAS IT. THAT WAS ALL OF IT."
2.24		Kelly:"WERE YOU THERE?"
2.25 1/3		Lorrie: " NO, I WAS ▮▮▮ WORKING IN ▮▮ CHICAGO."
2.31 2/3		She stops and tries to pull herself together.
2.33 2/3		Lorrie: "SCOTTY, ..."
2.35 2/3		Scotty leans over to her.
2.37		Scotty,starting to kneel down beside her,-"Listen, WE WON'T TALK ABOUT IT. ALRIGHT?"
2.40		Lorrie: "LOOK, I DON'T WANT TO BE RUDE BUT I HAVE ANOTHER SHOW TO DO."
2.48 2/3		Scotty nods.
2.51		He gives her a light kiss.
2.52		Scotty: "WE'LL SEE YOU LATER." (ends at 2.52 2/3)
2.52 2/3		Scotty starts to standup.
2.53 2/3		He walks over to Kelly.
2.56 2/3		As Scotty starts to exit, Kelly starts to follow and says "GOODNIGHT LORRIE."
2.58 1/3		Cut, medium shot K and S walking towards door.
3.00 1/3		Kelly opens door.
3.02		Scotty doesn't move. He is checking his pockets.
3.02		Kelly:"WHAT'S THE MATTER"
3.04 1/2		Scotty starts back in the room still checking his pockets.

(continued)

EXAMPLE #38 (Cont.)

"ISPY" # 30

M-33(Continued, page 4)

M33A

3.08	Scotty, as he approaches Lorrie: "ALRIGHT - GIVE ME IT BACK."
3.11	She looks up at him.
3.12	Lorrie:"HAVE YOU FLIPPED OR SOMETHING - GIVE WHAT BACK."
3.13 2/3	Scotty:"THE CODE BOOK, I HAD A CODE BOOK WHEN I CAME IN HERE AND I DON'T HAVE IT NOW. ALL THAT HUGGING AND KISSIN' WE'VE BEEN DOIN ----"
3.19	Lorrie, turns and gets up to face him.
3.19 13/	Scotty:(continued) " ...AND THEN YOU SLIPPED THE CODE BOOK OUT OF HERE. YOU'VE GOT PRETTY LIGHT FINGERS HAVEN'T YOU?" (ends: 3.22)
3.22	Lorrie slaps him right across the face.
3.22 2/3	They begin struggling.
3.22 2/3	scotty:"LISTEN -- LISTEN -- GIVE IT BACK."
3.26	Cut, med shot Kelly, stepping forward."HOLD IT - WHAT USE HAS SHE GOT FOR A CODE BOOK?"
3.28	Cut, medium shot, Lorrie and scotty still struggling. Scotty:"I DON'T KNOW BUT I CAME IN HERE WITH A CODE BOOK AND I DON'T HAVE ONE NOW. NOW GIVE IT BACK."
3.32 1/3	Cut, close shot, Kelly.
3.32 1/2	He grabs Scotty's arm.
3.32 2/3	Kelly:"THAT'S ENOUGH - COME ON, COOL IT - THAT IS ENOUGH." (ends: 3.34 2/3)
3.34	Kelly gets between Scotty and Lorrie.
3.35 2/3	Lorrie,upset,:"GET OUT OF HERE."
3.37 1/2	Kelly grabs Scotty and they start for the door.
3.40	Kelly stops half way to the door and turns to Lorrie
3.41 1/2	Kelly:"A - I'M SORRY LORRIE BUT MY STUPID FRIEND HAS LOST HIS CODE BOOK AND WE'VE GOT TO FIND IT."

(contineud)

EXAMPLE #38 (Cont.)

"I SPY" # 30

M-33 (Continued, page 5)

M33A

3.48	KELLY(Continued as he starts looking around room):
	"BECAUSE MY STUPID FRIEND HAS NOT GOT ENOUGH SENSE TO LEAVE IT IN THE MOTEL WHERE IT BELONGS --- LET'S SEE, YOU WERE OVER THERE - YOU CAME OVER HERE -- AND, AH -- " (Ends: 3.58)
3.58 1/2	He looks back in the closet.
4.01	He starts to bend down.
4.012/3	He picks up what ever it is he sees. He starts to get back up.
4.04 1/3	He turns around and we see he has the code book in his hand.
4.08 1/3	He starts ▓▓▓ back to Scotty.
4.12	Kelly to Scotty:" THIS WHAT YOU'RE LOOKING FOR?"
4.13 1/3	He hands it to Scotty.
4.16	Cut, close shot, Lorrie.
	DON'T
4.17 1/3	Lorrie:" WHY/YOU JUST TAKE IT AND GET OUT."
4.21 2/3	Cut, medium close shot, K & S.
4.26 2/3	Scotty:"LORRIE I COULD STAND HERE FOR ▓▓▓▓ TWENTY MINUTES AND SAY THE SAME THING OVER AND ▓▓▓ OVER, BUT I'M SORRY, PLEASE FORGIVE ME."
4.39 1/3	Cut, close shot, Lorrie.
4.41	Lorrie: " O,K." "O.K. SCOTTY"
4.45	Cut, full shot as Kelly opens the door.
4.49 1/2	They start out.
4.53 1/3	They close door behind them.
4.53. 1/2	Lorrie starts across the room.▓▓▓▓▓▓
4.56	She picks up the telephone ...
4.57	and begins to dial. End ▓▓▓▓ offstage source as she dials the telephone. (E.O.R. 500 1/3)

TOTAL TIME: 4.57

Technique #2 — SOURCE SCORING

Source scoring is one of the most valuable techniques in the picture business. This kind of music is like source in its content, but tailored to meet scoring requirements. It can drift in or out of tempo as you desire. It can contain lengthy thematic settings and yet catch few picture cues. The trick is to make it catch enough picture cues—naturally—to make it a combination of source and scoring. Example #35 shows a well-designed cue of this type. You can see by the cue sheets that principal points of action are caught by musical phrases. Once the main theme sets in at bar 13 in a trombone solo, the music plays the scene in a source-like setting and changes to pure scoring at bar 29. The start of this cue is in the sense of pure light scoring. You enter because you feel that it is dramatically right. Once in, the cue shifts into a source scoring setting and covers the bulk of the scene with a simple but totally effective setting. This kind of cue can start as pure source music and change over to source scoring. The main difference between Source and Source Scoring is that source scoring takes on a much closer relationship to the film. It follows the framework of the scene more critically and matches the nuances of the scene musically. It is closer to scoring in intent, but related to source in content. The exposition of a principal theme such as "Moon River," and "The Shadow Of Your Smile," lend themselves beautifully to the technique of source scoring. Entire pictures of contemporary nature are being scored with this technique. Sometimes the theme is set up in the main title of the picture with a vocal. From then on, it is used throughout the picture either with or without the vocal. Pictures scored in this fashion are usually monothematic. That does not necessarily mean that there will be no other music in the picture, but the bulk of the picture will be covered by a principal theme set in a popular fashion and tailored to meet the scoring requirements.

The deciding factor in the use of source scoring is the picture itself. If it lends itself to this kind of technique as a style of scoring the whole picture, by all means use it. If the whole picture cannot be carried by source scoring, look for those scenes in the picture where it can work effectively.

Technique #3 — PURE DRAMATIC SCORING — CLOSED OR OPEN

Pure scoring, or Dramatic scoring, is the granddaddy of the three principal techniques. The moment you make an entrance, you are in the realm of theatrics. It is usually difficult to get the novice to think in terms of theatrics, but that basically is what film music is about.

There is no literal qualification to pure scoring. The first note you play represents total dramatic license and you are writing music for a scene because, emotionally, you must. Pure scoring is the medium in which you get to express total creativity. How you feel about music, what you have to say musically, and your personal expression in the natural idiom you wish to use are all brought to fruition in pure scoring.

Closed scoring indicates that there is dialogue in the scene and there does exist some limitation of level and orchestra strength. The fine film composer can express himself with ease in and out of dialogue. Don't forget, you are playing the scene because you feel you have to. Whether the scene reflects tragedy, comedy, hysteria, or any other human emotion, you have elected to play it. You have taken on the responsibility of playing the scene; to help it register its impact for whatever emotional value it has and you cannot divorce yourself from any of the problems that the scene may contain.

In order to be successful in dramatic scoring, you must be able to relive the scene as you are working on it. The cue sheet that tells you in seconds what is happening on the screen must be alive, alive to your sense of recall in terms of emotional content.

Each word, each sentence, each silence, each look, each nuance, must be understood and assimilated by you, the composer, before you can successfully write the scene. You must have an overall objective and plan ahead to satisfy that objective. The faculty of absorbing the intent and necessities pertinent to composing music for films can and should be developed.

There are composers who can run a reel once and tell you in detail what the entire reel contained, cut by cut, word by word, and every shade of nuance in overall terms and minute specifics. This is a developed technique. It indicates that these particular composers have objectively learned to watch their picture for picture values and can harness the anxiety to think first in musical values. You cannot and should not think in terms of music when first watching a picture unless you have that rare ability to absorb all of the picture information at first sight. If you have that ability, well and good. If not, work hard at developing it. Any time you hear an unsuccessful score, or cue, you can be sure that the composer didn't know his picture. Learn what the film is about—and then trust it. Try to make yourself recognize not only what is strong in the film, but also what is weak.

Concentrate on photographic procedures. They can be the springboard to stunning musical effects. Make every bit of time that you spend in a projection room or over a Moviola pay off in terms of expanding your understanding of picture values and the mechanics of how these values are put together. The time to worry about music is when you are actually involved in the physical process of composing. Whenever you see a picture in a theatre or on T.V., try to figure out why the composer did what he did. Not how—why? How he did it goes into the area of music and when you get into that area you are on your own.

Open Scoring indicates no dialogue. It also means that there is no limitation as to orchestra strength, color, weight, or any other musical value. The only limitation is that the music must fit the picture and reflect what you see. There is no point in a long and specific dissertation on open scoring. The limitations on the composer have been stated and restated many times over up to this point in this book. Open scoring removes all of the limitations. Know what your film is about and what commentary you are going to make—and let go.

THE PSYCHOLOGY OF CREATING MUSIC
FOR FILMS

Example #39 shows both types of scoring in one cue. The beginning of this cue starts on an overlap from a preceding section. It starts open and then goes closed (under dialogue) near the end, and then finishes open again. As you see by the cue sheet, the cue grows to a climax at 2:49-1/3rd, builds to an even greater climax at 3:15-2/3rds, drops under dialogue at 3:31 1/2 and then continues quietly and ends softly and reflectively to fit the scene.

For pure scoring, every mechanical technique discussed in this book can be brought into play. Clicks—clicks and free timing—free timing only—overlaps—all can be freely used to facilitate the end result of dramatic scoring. To reproduce scores containing all of the combinations of usages possible would take volumes; they would have to be as varied as music itself, and as long as one new composer comes along who has something to say, you could never, by example, cover it all.

EXAMPLE #39

I SPY #43

M-26/31 (P. 3.)

1:34 1/2	Tonia: " NO, WE ARE NOT, IT WILL BE A SEMINAR, A DISCUSSION PERIOD." (Ends 1:38 1/2)
1:39 1/2	Scott: " O.K., ANYTHING YOU SAY - 'COURSE YA KNOW YOU'RE NOT GONNA FOOL THE ANTS. " (Ends 1:42)
1:42	Cut to Two-Shot as they start away with cart.
1:42 1/2	She protests in Italian about his haste: " SE---, SEE---." (Ends 1:44 1/2)
1:47	They start carefully to carry cart down a long flight of steps.

End Cty.

1:51 1/3 →1:54 3/4	Cut to Start of Rec/3 as Scott & Tonia are coming down Spanish Steps toward camera from a L.S.
1:56	Start Dissolve.

M 26/31 A | 1:58 OVERLAP

1:58	Full In on M.S. Scott & Tonia sitting on wall by river.
⊕ 2:04 2:06	She hops down from wall and beckons him to come along.
2:09 2/3	Start Dissolve.
2:11 2/3 ⊕ 2:14 2/3 2:15 2/3	Full In as S. & T. approach shop window. They stop to look.
2:18 ⊕2:18 2/3 2:21	While she bends to look at something, Scott disappears into the shop. She looks up but doesn't see Scott.
2:22 1/3 ⊕ 2:22 2/3 2:24 2/3	She looks about. Scott appears from behind.
⊕2:26 2/3 2:27 2/3	He presents her with a silk scarf.
2:29 ⊕ 2:30 2/3 2:34 2/3 2:38 2/3	He places it around her neck as she becomes happily embarrassed. She places a hand-kiss on his lips.
2:39 1/3	Start Dissolve
2:41 1/3 ⊕ 2:43 2/3	Full In on a Full Shot of S. & T. playing a kind of 'towel-tag' on the steps of a large building.
2:43 2/3 ⊕2:45 2/3 2:47 2/3	He siezes her around waist-both very happy. They sit on steps-she in his arms as he starts nuzzling up.
2:49 1/3	Start Dissolve

(cont'd.)

EXAMPLE #39   (Cont.)

I SPY #43

M-26/31 (F.4.)

2:51 1/3   Full In on a very bustling scene of pedestrians.

2:53   Camera starts moving in closer through the crowd.

2:55 1/4   Camera Stops Med. Close on Scott & Tonia in a
⊕2:59   tight smooching clinch completely oblivious of
                 the passing crowd that is also oblivious of them.

⊣(3:03)   Start Dissolve.

3:05   She says, "I DON'T KNOW, YOU'VE DONE SOMETHING
                 TO ME--I FEEL SO NEW." (Ends 3:09)

3:09   Cut to C.U. Scott-really smitten.

⊣(3:10 2/3)   Scott answers: "BECAUSE YOU WERE 'NEW' ALL
                 THE TIME." (Ends 3:12 2/3)

⊣(3:15 2/3)   They start to move slowly in for another big kiss.

3:18 1/3   They contact in big kiss.

3:21 1/3   Cut to Reverse Angle C.U. on Tonia-nussling
⊕3:22 1/3   and loving this kind of attention.

3:22 2/3   She says, happily gasping: "OH! THANK YOU, THANK
                 YOU! DIO TE BENE DICA." (Made 3:26 2/3)

3:27   Cut to M.C. Two-Shot.

3:27 1/4   Scott: "DON'T THANK ME, O.K.? JUST DON'T THANK
⊕3:24 1/3   ME!" (Ends 3:31 1/4)

3:31 1/4   He moves away toward door as though caught in
                 something he's undecided about.

3:35   Closes door behind him.

⊣(3:35 1/3)   Cut to CU Tonia-perplexed about S.'s sudden change.

3:42   She looks-a bit sadly now-down at the scarf he
                 gave her.

⊣(3:34 2/3)   Start Dissolve

3:45 2/3   Music Seques to M-33 as picture Full In on C.U.
                 bartender's hands serving two glasses on top
                 of bar.

TOTAL TIME   3:45 2/3

EXAMPLE #39 (Cont.)   Record Band #16

EXAMPLE #39 (Cont.)

BOOK III

THE RESPONSIBILITIES
OF
THE COMPOSER

In addition to writing music for the picture, the composer has other duties to accept and fulfill. These include pre-production planning, during-shooting coverage, and post-production performance. These functions are extremely important; if not handled properly they can affect the writing of the score itself. It is the intention of this book to completely cover the field of film music. Therefore, Book III deals with areas that may seem unrelated to the writing of a musical score; however, these functions are a necessary part of the whole, and, expected or not, serve as a contribution to a better end result.

If you are packaging the film and taking on the responsibility for delivering the score at a price, it's absolutely necessary that you know the information in this chapter. If you are unsure as to procedure, use this part of the book as a reference guide.

BOOK III

CHAPTER 1

PRE-FILMING PREPARATION

More and more, the composers are being consulted by the producer and/or the director for the proper methods of handling sticky problems in shooting that involve music. This is generally discussed on the basis of the script or production shooting schedule because the actual filming has not yet begun. Before you can discuss the pre-filming problems intelligently, you must first read and break down the script. Some films contain no pre-filming problems and others are loaded with them. It is the composers responsibility to categorize the problem areas, digest them, and come up with workable answers as to the methods to be used in shooting. In the motion picture field, the composer will probably have help in these areas. Generally a music cutter will be assigned to work on pre-production problems. Some studios, the majors in particular, have qualified, specialized help who deal specifically in these areas. The methods to be used, however, should be decided by the composer. After all, he is faced with the task of putting all of the product together in the final sense and he should have the authority to decide how all of the picture problems will be handled.

There is also the possibility that the composer may be working without any outside help at all and will have to live with any mistakes that are made in the pre-production planning. The time to cure mistakes is before they happen. Later on, it can get expensive both in time and money. No matter how specific you may be with the production company in terms of helping the final problem, there might still be mistakes made and you can often find yourself faced with some nasty problems that will require endless time and trouble to overcome.

The first step is to mark out the script. As you read the script through, bend down the corner of any pages that may involve visual music. After you have read the whole script, go back to the pages that involve music and analyze each problem separately. Break down your <u>pre-filming</u>, or <u>pre-production</u> work into these categories:

1. Pre-recording

2. Orchestra guide tracks

3. Tempo tracks

4. Legal clearances

<u>Production</u> (during shooting) problems will fall in these categories:

1. Lip synch of pre-recording

2. Standard recording on the stage

3. Sideline musicians

4. Playback procedures for guide tracks

<u>Post-production</u> (after shooting) problems fall into these categories:

1. Assembly of pre-recorded tracks

2. Breakdown preparation for scoring

3. Hiring of orchestra personnel

4. Physical recording of all music

5. Preparation of cue sheets

6. Preparation of all music tracks for dubbing

7. Dubbing procedures

8. Preview or answer print attendance

9. Re-composing or re-cutting music if the picture is changed after preview or answer print running

This is the total list of the responsibilities of the film composer.

If it seems endless for someone who is essentially a composer, be assured that all of these functions have to be covered. If the studio provides any help along these lines then your work will be commensurately lessened. You should, however, be prepared to take charge of any function involving music. This list of responsibilities is vital to the picture business and valuable enough to be discussed in detail. The majority of the list pertains to mechanics rather than aesthetics; so we will examine them one by one.

PRE-PRODUCTION PLANNING

After you have broken down the script for pre-production problems a great deal of conversation is indicated. A good rapport with the director of the picture is essential to enable the two of you to plan procedures that will not complicate the shooting or the final product. It is to your common benefit that any problems in pre-production be resolved before the start of the actual filming. Very often, the ideal solution for you will inhibit the director. It pays to study each of the problems involved and have alternate procedures available. Occasionally, you will come into contact with a director who not only doesn't understand the nature of musical problems, but furthermore doesn't want to. If you cannot convince him that your interests are common, you are just going to have to make up your mind to accept an end product that is less than practical and do the best you can with it. This situation, fortunately, doesn't happen too often. When it does, you have no alternative but to repair it one way or another. With the great variety of mechanics at your disposal, there is no situation that you cannot repair. You will often find yourself repairing a job that you have declared impractical. The successful repair jobs sometimes has an inverse effect on the producing personnel. They wonder why all of the fuss in the first place when the end result turned out fine. The answer is that there was twice as much time spent, or more, in repairing the job when there was an easier way of doing it in the first place. This answer, logical and correct as it may be, will generally fall on deaf ears. The end result is what counts, so prepare yourself to be flexible when people with whom you work are not.

PRE-PRODUCTION PROCEDURES

#1 LEGAL CLEARANCES

Every piece of music with the exception of P.D. (public domain) material, is owned by someone. The copyright holder has the right to charge a synchronization fee and/or a performance fee for the usage of his copyright. Before you can perform a copyrighted piece of material, you must have a license from the copyright holder, or publisher stating the price he is going to charge for the usage involved. In the film business, the price is based on an exactly stated usage. For example, the price for one chorus of vocal and eight bars of orchestra might be half of the price for two choruses of vocal and eight bars of orchestra. Besides this synch price, the publisher will generally charge a performance fee. Motion picture theaters do not pay performance rights to the performing rights societies, so the producer must pay the publisher directly. In T.V., there is almost no synch fee asked, and no performance money due as the networks and stations do pay performance money to both the publisher and the composer. The performance rights collection societies are complicated in structure. Information regarding the two major performance societies, A.S.C.A.P. (American Society of Composers And Publishers) and B.M.I. (Broadcast Music Inc.) may be had by writing to ASCAP, 575 Madison Ave., New York City, N.Y. 10022, or B.M.I., 589 Fifth Ave., New York City, N.Y. 10017.

If you are going to make a career out of composition for public performance, it is vital to belong to one of these performance rights societies. They exist to collect performance monies all over the world for their publisher and composer members.

While it is not the direct responsibility of the composer to furnish musical legal services, the question of legal clearance should be asked and answered. You might assume that a piece of music is P.D. and find out that it is not. To use music in a film without getting a license is to ask for a suit. The major film studios have legal departments to handle the problems of clearances. All T.V. networks have music legal departments. If you are working with an independent company, you can do yourself and your producer a service by making sure that all material to be recorded, even if an artist claims it to be original, be accompanied by an acceptable legal clearance.

By the same token, each cue that you write must have a title and a separate clearance sheet. These cue sheets are generally made up by the picture companies' legal department. The cue sheets should have the name of the picture, the production number, the title of the music cue, the proper name of the composer, and the performance society, if any, to which you belong.

If you are working for a small indepedent organization, by all means try to secure the publishing rights. Over a period of time, the publishing rights can add to your income from performance fees. If you obtain the publishing rights, you must provide the producing organization or producer with cue sheets and legal clearance to indemnify him from suit on the music you deem original.

To copyright any specific theme, you must obtain a copy of the "E" copyright form, attach a lead sheet to it and send it to the Register of Copyrights office, Washington, D.C. One form must be used for each piece of material. If the theme has lyrics that you wish to protect, put them on the lead sheet. The price for copyrighting in the U.S. is $6.00. The copyright that you secure from the U.S. also protects you in any country with whom the U.S. has a copyright treaty. Great Britain, France, Australia, etc. are all covered by your U.S. copyright. In the case of International copyrights for the film company's protection, have a complete list of cues and their titles made out for the specific film and have the picture company secure International copyright when they apply for it for the film. Be sure and list all of the titles, including the ones you have secured on separate form "E" copyrights. The first 4 sections of the "E" form are the sections that pertain to your music. They are self-explanatory.

At this point, the author feels the necessity of inserting a word of caution!

Your job as a composer is to furnish your client with an <u>original</u> score for his film. The word "original" has many implications to it. There are many people who claim that no music written today either in the film industry, the record industry, or the concert hall, is purely and absolutely original. Each of us, however, within the framework of his creativity, has the obligation to keep the music as original as possible. You must keep in mind that the composer and the publisher who represents his music are liable for suit if there is an infringement on the copyrighted material of any other composer.

If you are hired to develop, arrange, or compose music based on the material of another composer, (songs, for example) so long as the film company has purchased or received the rights to use that

EXAMPLE #40

"THE MOD SQUAD" - #26
"A Seat By The Window"

Thomas/Spelling Prods.
ABC-TV -- 4/15/69

MUSIC CLEARANCE SHEET

	TITLE OF MUSIC	COMPOSER	PUBLISHER	TIME	PERFORMANCE LICENSOR
	BUMPER	HAGEN	EDJ MUSIC	:05	BMI
	LEAVE THE DRIVING TO US	MAY	EDJ	:27	BMI
	ONE OF OUR GUYS	MAY	EDJ	:44	BMI
	MAIN TITLE MUSIC:				
	MOD SQUAD MAIN TITLE	HAGEN	EDJ	:54	BMI
	WHAT'S HAPPENING?	MAY	EDJ	:25	BMI
	TIAJUANA BUS	MAY	EDJ	:27	BMI
	NO THANKS, FELLOWS	MAY	EDJ	:21	BMI
	DIDN'T SPILL A DROP	MAY	EDJ	:52	BMI
**	FRICK AND FRACK FESTIVAL	BRANDT	EDJ	:46	BMI
**	TRUMPET WARM-UP	BRANDT	EDJ	:44	BMI
*	THIS IS MY WOMAN	BERNSTEIN/ MILLROSE	FAMOUS MUSIC	1:01	ASCAP
	DIRTY ROCK	HAGEN	EDJ	1:55	BMI
	PRETTY	HAGEN	EDJ	1:51	BMI
	PLAIN FUNK	HAGEN	EDJ	1:45	BMI
	PLAYOFF	BRANDT	EDJ	:05	BMI
**	CHICKEN FLICKIN'	BRANDT	EDJ	1:45	BMI
*	TROUBLE IN MIND	R. JONES	LEEDS MUSIC	1:23	ASCAP
**	UNWASHED SONATA	BRANDT	EDJ	:18	BMI
**	LITTLE BLONDE	BRANDT	EDJ	:24	BMI
**	CAPO BLUES	BRANDT	EDJ	:54	BMI
	JIGGERS THE FUZZ	HAGEN	EDJ	:57	BMI
	DEPOSIT TEN CENTS	MAY	EDJ	1:16	BMI
	BUMPER	HAGEN	EDJ	:05	BMI
**	IRON BLUES	HAGEN	EDJ	2:17	BMI
	COUNTRY GIRL	HAGEN	EDJ	4:09	BMI
	DISCOVERED	HAGEN	EDJ	:44	BMI
	PLEASE,MA'M,THATAWAY	MAY	EDJ	1:03	BMI
	ON YUMUS STINGGER	MAY	EDJ	:31	BMI
	RUN,TOM,RUN	MAY	EDJ	1:09	BMI
	WOW, CAN YOU BELIEVE?	MAY	EDJ	1:10	BMI
	T.S. WILLA	HAGEN/BRANDT	EDJ	:32	BMI
	BE HAPPY, YOU MODDERS	HAGEN	EDJ	:23	BMI
	END TITLE MUSIC:				
	MOD SQUAD END TITLE	HAGEN	EDJ	:41	BMI

NOTE: * VISUAL VOCAL
      ** VISUAL INSTRUMENTAL
   All other music uses are background instrumental.

EXAMPLE #41

DANNY THOMAS PRODUCTIONS

ABC-TV   --   9/30/70

MAKE ROOM FOR GRANDDADDY

EP # 008 - "THE RETURN OF BARNEY SHAKER"

TELEVISION MUSIC CLEARANCE
CUE SHEET

TITLE OF MUSIC	COMPOSER	PUBLISHER	PERFORMANCE TIME	LICENSOR
MAIN TITLE MUSIC:				
LONDONDERRY AIR	TRAD., ARR. BY HAGEN	E.D.J.	0:54	BMI
ALL'S QUIET	HAGEN	E.D.J.	0:18	BMI
* TEA FOR TWO	YOUMANS, CAESAR	WARNER BROS. MUSIC	0:16	ASCAP
** LIVING THE LIFE I LOVE	FAIN, SEELER	WARNER BROS. MUSIC	1:32	ASCAP
BROKE	HAGEN	E.D.J.	0:45	BMI
** NATURE BOY	AHBEZ	CRESTVIEW	0:37	ASCAP
THAT'S ALL	HAGEN	E.D.J.	0:20	BMI
THAT'S ALL #2	HAGEN	E.D.J.	0:19	BMI
** MERRY-GO-ROUND BROKE DOWN	FRIEND, FRANKLIN	WARNER BROS. MUSIC	0:11	ASCAP
LITTLE MAN	HAGEN	E.D.J.	0:15	BMI
NO CHANCE	HAGEN	E.D.J.	0:10	BMI
* BLUES VAMP	G. RHODES	E.D.J.	0:06	BMI
BUM THROAT	HAGEN	E.D.J.	0:18	BMI
** WITHOUT A SONG	ROSE, ELISCU, YOUMANS	MILLER/ANNE-RACHEL	0:39	ASCAP
HERE IS DE PLACE	HAGEN	E.D.J.	1:48	BMI
END CREDIT MUSIC:				
LONDONDERRY AIR	TRAD., ARR. BY HAGEN	E.D.J.	0:08	BMI
LONDONDERRY AIR	TRAD., ARR. BY HAGEN	E.D.J.	0:37	BMI

NOTE: *   VISUAL INSTRUMENTAL
         **   VISUAL VOCAL

ALL THE OTHER MUSIC USES ARE BACKGROUND INSTRUMENTAL.

EXAMPLE #42

Page 1

FORM E

Application for Registration of a Claim to Copyright

in a musical composition the author of which is a citizen or domiciliary of the United States of America or which was first published in the United States of America

CLASS	REGISTRATION NO.
E	DO NOT WRITE HERE
	EP EU

Instructions: Make sure that all applicable spaces have been completed before you submit the form. The application must be **SIGNED** at line 9. For published works the application should not be submitted until after the date of publication given in line 4(a), and should state the facts which existed on that date. For further information, see page 4.

Pages 1 and 2 should be typewritten or printed with pen and ink. Pages 3 and 4 should contain exactly the same information as pages 1 and 2, but may be carbon copies.

Mail all pages of the application to the Register of Copyrights, Library of Congress, Washington, D.C. 20540, together with:

(a) If unpublished, one complete copy of the work and the registration fee of $6.

(b) If published, two copies of the best edition of the work and the registration fee of $6.

Make your remittance payable to the Register of Copyrights.

1. Copyright Claimant(s) and Address(es): Give the name(s) and address(es) of the copyright owner(s). In the case of published works the name(s) should ordinarily be the same as in the notice of copyright on the copies deposited.

Name _____

Address _____

Name _____

Address _____

2. Title: _____
(Give the title of the musical composition as ft appears on the copies)

_____

3. Authors: Citizenship and domicile information must be given. Where a work is made for hire, the employer is the author. Organizations formed under U.S. Federal or State law are U.S. citizens.

Authors include composers of music, authors of words, arrangers, compilers, etc. If the copyright claim is based on new matter (see line 5) give information about the author of the new matter.

Name _____ Citizenship: U.S.A. _____ Other _____
(Give legal name followed by pseudonym if latter appears on the copies)   (Check if U.S. citizen)   (Name of country)

Domiciled in U.S.A. Yes ____ No ____ Address _____ Author of _____
    (State which: words, music, arrangement, etc.)

Name _____ Citizenship: U.S.A. _____ Other _____
(Give legal name followed by pseudonym if latter appears on the copies)   (Check if U.S. citizen)   (Name of country)

Domiciled in U.S.A. Yes ____ No ____ Address _____ Author of _____
    (State which: words, music, arrangement, etc.)

Name _____ Citizenship: U.S.A. _____ Other _____
(Give legal name followed by pseudonym if latter appears on the copies)   (Check if U.S. citizen)   (Name of country)

Domiciled in U.S.A. Yes ____ No ____ Address _____ Author of _____
    (State which: words, music, arrangement, etc.)

➤➤ **NOTE:** | **Leave all spaces of line 4 blank unless your work has been PUBLISHED.** | ◄◄

4. (a) Date of Publication: Give the date when copies of this particular version of the work were first placed on sale, sold, or publicly distributed. The date when copies were made or printed, or the date when the work was performed should not be confused with the date of publication. NOTE: The full date (month, day, and year) must be given.

_____
    (Month)   (Day)   (Year)

(b) Place of Publication: Give the name of the country in which this particular version of the work was first published.

_____

➤➤ **NOTE:** | **Leave all spaces of line 5 blank unless the instructions below apply to your work.** | ◄◄

5. Previous Registration or Publication: If a claim to copyright in any substantial part of this work was previously registered in the U.S. Copyright Office in unpublished form, or if any substantial part of the work was previously published anywhere, give requested information.

Was work previously registered? Yes _____ No _____ Date of registration _____ Registration number _____

Was work previously published? Yes _____ No _____ Date of publication _____ Registration number _____

Is there any substantial **NEW MATTER** in this version? Yes .... No .... If your answer is "Yes," give a brief general statement of the nature of the **NEW MATTER** in this version. (New matter may consist of compilation, arrangement, adaptation, editorial revision, and the like, as well as additional words and music.)

EXAMINER

Complete all applicable spaces on next page

EXAMPLE #42 (Cont.)

6. If registration fee is to be charged to a deposit account established in the Copyright Office, give name of account:

----

7. Name and address of person or organization to whom correspondence or refund, if any, should be sent:

Name _____ Address _____

8. Send certificate to:

(Type or print name and address)

Name _____

Address _____
(Number and street)

_____
(City)   (State)   (ZIP code)

9. Certification:

(Application not acceptable unless signed)

I CERTIFY that the statements made by me in this application are correct to the best of my knowledge.

_____
(Signature of copyright claimant or duly authorized agent)

Application Forms

Copies of the following forms will be supplied by the Copyright Office without charge upon request.

Class A — Form A—Published book manufactured in the United States of America.

Class A or B
- Form A–B Foreign—Book or periodical manufactured outside the United States of America (except works subject to the ad interim provisions of the copyright law).
- Form A–B Ad Interim—Book or periodical in the English language manufactured and first published outside the United States of America.

Class B
- Form B—Periodical manufactured in the United States of America.
- Form BB—Contribution to a periodical manufactured in the United States of America.

Class C — Form C—Lecture or similar production prepared for oral delivery.

Class D — Form D—Dramatic or dramatico-musical composition.

Class E
- Form E—Musical composition the author of which is a citizen or domiciliary of the United States of America or which was first published in the United States of America.
- Form E Foreign—Musical composition the author of which is not a citizen or domiciliary of the United States of America and which was not first published in the United States of America.

Class F — Form F—Map.

Class G — Form G—Work of art or a model or design for a work of art.

Class H — Form H—Reproduction of a work of art.

Class I — Form I—Drawing or plastic work of a scientific or technical character.

Class J — Form J—Photograph.

Class K
- Form K—Print or pictorial illustration.
- Form KK—Print or label used for an article of merchandise.

Class L or M — Form L–M—Motion picture.

Form R—Renewal copyright.

Form U—Notice of use of copyrighted music on mechanical instruments.

FOR COPYRIGHT OFFICE USE ONLY	
Application received	
One copy received	
Two copies received	
Fee received	
Renewal	

Page 3

Certificate
Registration of a Claim to Copyright

in a musical composition the author of which is a citizen or domiciliary of the United States of America or which was first published in the United State of America

This Is To Certify that the statements set forth in this certificate have been made a part of the records of the Copyright Office. In witness whereof the seal of the Copyright Office is hereto affixed.

Register of Copyrights
United States of America

CLASS	REGISTRATION NO.
E	DO NOT WRITE HERE

FORM E

NOT VALID WITHOUT COPYRIGHT OFFICE IMPRESSION SEAL

1. Copyright Claimant(s) and Address(es):

Name --

Address ---

Name --

Address ---

2. Title: --
(Title of the musical composition)

----

3. Authors:

Name --- Citizenship: U.S.A. ------ Other ------------------------
(Legal name followed by pseudonym if latter appears on the copies)   (Check if U.S. citizen)   (Name of country)

Domiciled in U.S.A. Yes ---- No ---- Address -- Author of ------------------------
(State which: words, music, arrangement, etc.)

Name --- Citizenship: U.S.A. ------ Other ------------------------
(Legal name followed by pseudonym if latter appears on the copies)   (Check if U.S. citizen)   (Name of country)

Domiciled in U.S.A. Yes ---- No ---- Address -- Author of ------------------------
(State which: words, music, arrangement, etc.)

Name --- Citizenship: U.S.A. ------ Other ------------------------
(Legal name followed by pseudonym if latter appears on the copies)   (Check if U.S. citizen)   (Name of country)

Domiciled in U.S.A. Yes ---- No ---- Address -- Author of ------------------------
(State which: words, music, arrangement, etc.)

4. (a) Date of Publication:

(Month)   (Day)   (Year)

(b) Place of Publication:

(Name of country)

5. Previous Registration or Publication:

Was work previously registered? Yes ----- No ----- Date of registration ------------------- Registration number -------------------

Was work previously published? Yes ----- No ----- Date of publication ------------------- Registration number -------------------

Is there any substantial **NEW MATTER** in this version? Yes ------ No ------ If your answer is "Yes," give a brief general statement of the nature of the **NEW MATTER** in this version.

EXAMINER

Complete all applicable spaces on next page

EXAMPLE #42 (Cont.)

6. Deposit account:

---

7. Send correspondence to:

Name _____   Address _____

8. Send certificate to:

(Type or
print
name and
address)

Name _____

Address _____
(Number and street)

_____
(City)   (State)   (ZIP code)

Information concerning copyright in musical compositions

When to Use Form E. Form E is appropriate for unpublished and published musical compositions by authors who are U.S. citizens or domiciliaries, and for musical compositions first published in the United States.

What Is a "Musical Composition"? The term "musical composition" includes compositions consisting of music alone, or of words and music combined. It also includes arrangements and other versions of earlier compositions, if new copyrightable work of authorship has been added.

—*Song Lyrics Alone.* The term "musical composition" does not include song poems and other works consisting of words without music. Works of that type are not registrable for copyright in unpublished form.

—*Sound Recordings.* Phonograph records, tape recordings, and other sound recordings are not regarded as "copies" of the musical compositions recorded on them, and are not acceptable for copyright registration. For purposes of deposit, the musical compositions should be written in some form of legible notation. If the composition contains words, they should be written above or beneath the notes to which they are sung.

Duration of Copyright. Statutory copyright begins on the date the work was first published, or, if the work was registered for copyright in unpublished form, copyright begins on the date of registration. In either case, copyright lasts for 28 years, and may be renewed for a second 28-year term.

Unpublished musical compositions

How to Register a Claim. To obtain copyright registration, mail to the Register of Copyrights, Library of Congress, Washington, D.C. 20540, one complete copy of the musical composition, an application Form E, properly completed and signed, and a fee of $6. Manuscripts are not returned so do not send your only copy.

Procedure to Follow if Work Is Later Published. If the work is later reproduced in copies and published, it is necessary to make a second registration, following the procedure outlined below. To maintain copyright protection, all copies of the published edition must contain a copyright notice in the required form and position.

Published musical compositions

What Is "Publication"? Publication, generally, means the sale, placing on sale, or public distribution of copies. Limited distribution of so-called "professional" copies ordinarily would not constitute publication. However, since the dividing line between a preliminary distribution and actual publication may be difficult to determine, it is wise for the author to affix notice of copyright to copies that are to be circulated beyond his control.

How to Secure Copyright in a Published Musical Composition:
1. *Produce copies with copyright notice,* by printing or other means of reproduction.
2. *Publish the work.*
3. *Register the copyright claim,* following the instructions on page 1 of this form.

The Copyright Notice. In order to secure and maintain copyright protection for a published work, it is essential that all copies published in the United States contain the statutory copyright notice. This notice shall appear on the title page or first page of music and must consist of three elements:

1. *The word "Copyright," the abbreviation "Copr.," or the symbol* ©. Use of the symbol © may result in securing copyright in countries which are parties to the Universal Copyright Convention.

2. *The year date of publication.* This is ordinarily the date when copies were first placed on sale, sold, or publicly distributed. However, if the work has been registered for copyright in unpublished form, the notice should contain the year of registration; or, if there is new copyrightable matter in the published version, it should include both dates.

3. *The name of the copyright owner (or owners).* Example: © John Doe 1969.

NOTE: If copies are published without the required notice the right to secure copyright is lost and cannot be restored.

FOR COPYRIGHT OFFICE USE ONLY	
Application received	
One copy received	
Two copies received	
Fee received	

composer's music, you are not liable in any way.

The other exception to the rule is when you use material that is in the Public Domain. I caution you not to <u>assume</u> that material is P.D. Before you use it, know it to be fact. There are many P.D. songs that have been copyrighted by the addition of a lyric. For example; the P.D. song, "Good Morning, Dear Teacher" remains in the Public Domain—however, the lyric, "Happy Birthday To You," which has been written for this piece of material is copyrighted. Any usage of "Good Morning, Dear Teacher," which implies a birthday sequence constitutes an infringement on the copyright of "Happy Birthday To You" by intent. Your usage of it makes the producer liable for a synchronization fee. If you are not sure that the music you intend to use, or base your score upon, is P.D., then I suggest one of the following procedures: If there is a major network radio or television station near you, the chances are that they will have a music library. A call to that librarian can possibly answer your questions. If no such facility is available to you, a letter to one of the major performance societies (B.M.I. or A.S.C.A.P.) may get you your answer. A letter to the music division of the Library of Congress can also get you invaluable information.

Make every effort possible to authenticate the fact that any material you wish to use or base your score upon is in the Public Domain before you use this music. Any arrangement, development, or setting that you create makes it your composition. It should be listed on the cue sheet under its P.D. name as arranged by you. This automatically entitles you to collect performances on this material.

If you are working in the area of original music and you have the slightest doubt that what you are writing is original, write something else!

If you feel that the music is even vaguely similar to something else, write another piece of music.

Once your name appears on a cue sheet as the composer of a piece of material, you are deemed to be the creator of that music.

Make sure that you really are.

#2—PRE-RECORDING

Practically all vocals, dance routines, or combinations of vocals and dance routines should be pre-recorded whenever possible. The advantages of pre-recording vocals are enormous although the artist is faced with lip synch (matching his or her lip movements, while being photographed, to the pre-recorded words). If a vocal is pre-recorded, there does not have to be any close microphone pickup. This means that the director can pull his camera back at any point without disclosing the boom microphones that are used to record dialogue on the stage. Pre-recorded vocals assure you of the best possible vocal result. You can cut as many vocal tracks together as you need to get a good master track. This master track can also be used by the director to shoot his master shot. By having a "stop and go" playback machine on the filming stage, the director can make any kind of shot he likes from long shot to close up and know that they can be cut into the final print without having any editing problems. The "stop-and-go" playback machine is a synch pulse turntable that has a trigger-operated start and stop button on a remote lead. The final vocal take is transferred from film to two 33-1/3rd, r.p.m. discs, one for use and one for protection. This disc can be marked with a white grease pencil for starts by the playback operator. Some production companies are now using synch pulse ¼" tape recorders for playback procedures.

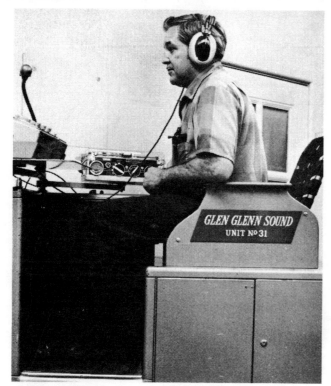

EXAMPLE #43
On-stage Dialogue
Recorder/Playback Console

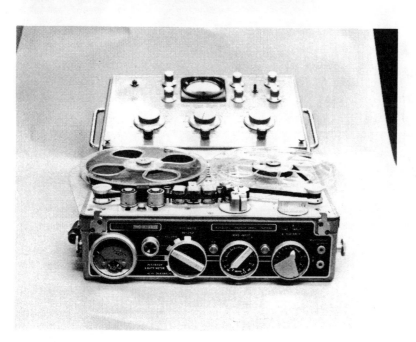

EXAMPLE #44   The ¼" Synch Pulse Recorder

Record   Synch   Playback
                Pulse

EXAMPLE #45   Head Configuration, 1/4 inch Tape Recorder

EXAMPLE #46   Magnification of Synch Pulse on 1/4 inch Tape

The procedure for photographing a pre-recorded vocal is that the director first shoots his master shot — start to finish, if possible. This can be in close up, medium shot, or long shot — whatever the director prefers. After he has established his master shot, he can move to other angles for additional cuts that he may wish to make. By selecting his cuts from the pre-recorded track, a start mark can be made on the disc or tape, and he can shoot the shot knowing that it will cut into the picture without disturbing the continuity of the music. From the standpoint of flexibility, pre-recording offers the director the widest latitude. It has other advantages. It eliminates the problem of trying to record with poor facilities. Film stages are not recording stages in the musical sense, and the problem of trying to get a recording balance is totally eliminated by pre-recording. Also, the human frailties of poor voice, poor orchestra performance, or both, are eliminated as well.

The director and you do not have to worry about getting a usable voice and orchestra track while extras, gaffers, wardrobe people, and hosts of others attached to physical production, sit around accumulating expensive hours.

The procedure of pre-recording usually starts with a meeting with the vocalist or choreographer. If the budget of your picture warrants the expense, it is ideal to have a separate recording session prior to the shooting date. It is always desireable to have a few days between the recording and the shooting. This gives the artist a chance to get a record of the vocal, or dance, and spend some time rehearsing to it for lip synch or body movements.

Once the orchestral arrangements are put into work, a stage should be booked, usually through the production company, and a call put out for the musicians.

Ideally, the best way to pre-record a vocal is to record the orchestra and vocalist separately. If the number allows, you would record the orchestra first, then the vocalist puts on a headset and records the vocal to the orchestra track. This puts the orchestra and the vocalist on separate tracks and allows the opportunity to make cuts from several takes and wind up with the very best that the artist can offer. In this case, the orchestra becomes your master track to cut to. It also allows you to get a better orchestra track. When making an orchestra track alone for later vocal over-dubbing, be very sure that you have enough rhythm and bass on the track. Don't forget that it will be under the vocal at a reduced level and the tendency when you listen to the orchestra track being played back is to settle for a balance without making allowances for the vocal. Once you and the artist O.K. the track, the orchestra is dismissed. If you have to make any further orchestral adjustments after you make the vocal, you are dead. All vocal takes are made to a common start mark and all of them are slated separately.

Obviously, the better way to record your orchestra and vocal tracks would be to use multi-track recording. If the studio isn't set up for 8-, 16-, 24- or 32-track recording, you can use as many three stripes as you need. This gives you the opportunity to do some post recording rebalancing.

Once you have a finished orchestra track and a finished vocal track, any necessary intercuts having been made, you then make a re-recorded combine of orchestra and vocal for stage playback. This combined track is generally recorded with the vocal at an abnormally high level to make it easier for the artist to lip synch. This temporary combine is transferred to 33 1/3 r.p.m. records, or 78 r.p.m. records for playback purposes on the stage. An additional study copy is given to the artist. Selected takes of the orchestra master and vocal master (intercut, if necessary) are carefully marked and stored until the final picture re-recording (Dubbing) when, along with all the rest of the sound and music tracks in the picture, they are re-recorded into their proper perspective.

If for any vocal reason, such as extreme rubato or inability on the part of the artist to work to headset, or whatever, you should attempt to get a Split Channel* set up. A split channel set up is where the artist is placed in a glass walled isolation booth. The music is piped to the artist over a low level speaker or a head set. The artist is piped to the conductor via headset. The artist and the conductor can see and hear each other and although they record simultaneously, the vocal is recorded on one piece of film and the orchestra on another. This method gives you the flexibility of separate tracks. It allows you to intercut, to make a set track with high artist level, and the possibility of sliding the vocal track or frame-cutting it to fit lip synch after the sequence is shot. Frame-cutting is exactly what it says. If the artist is not in dead lip synch, you can move single words forward or backwards to get them to fit the picture. You must always be sure to replace the piece of film, minute as it may be, after the word, or words, that you move! This keeps the vocal track in relative alignment with the orchestra. Obviously, if you do not have a separate vocal track you cannot do this kind of cutting. The jumps in the orchestra track would be immediately noticeable. You will find that most artists have a tendency to trail the playback when lip synching to a pre-recorded track. Most times, pulling the vocal or vocal and orchestra track up a hole or two will sharpen the whole product and cure the "rubbery" looking synch. Lip synching in most cases is not a large problem and most artists prefer the well recorded track and lip synch to trying to record while they are being photographed. Almost all live T.V. specials and variety shows pre-record their vocals and dance routines and go to the lip synch method.

If the split channel set up is not available, you will have to record under whatever circumstances you can get. If the best that you can get is a monaural set up, the only intercuts that you can make will have to accommodate both voice and orchestra. Your best out in these circumstances is to try for the best overall take you can get and avoid intercutting as much as possible.

If no budget is available to you to pre-record with orchestra, try still to pre-record with a temporary guide track. If the number is in tempo, by all means use clicks. All you need is a loop or two on both sides of the right tempo. If after rehearsing you decide to pick up the tempo slightly, or slow it down slightly, all you have to do is put up a faster or slower loop. A guide track background can be made with as little as piano only, but if the number is rhythmic, try to at least get a rhythm section.

See glossary

In your post scoring, you can retain the rhythm track and overdub the orchestra to it. If you have made the guide track background to a click, your problems are even more simple. The whole sequence can be laid out to the click and you can retain the guide track or abandon it entirely. If the number is rubato and you are faced with post scoring it, get yourself a record of the piano and voice to arrange to, and set up your post scoring with clicks, streamers, punches, or whatever mechanical means necessary to simplify your post-recording job. Try always to simplify post-scoring. Split the number into short segments that can be easily recorded, if necessary.

Review Example #27 for a similar set of circumstances. In this case, a great deal of the original number was cut out. This created some difficult circumstances which were overcome by a lot of Moviola time and a thoroughly sensible layout.

#3—GUIDE TRACKS AND TEMPO TRACKS

If there is any visual dancing to be shot in a scene, a guide track or tempo track should be provided. The guide track can be a commercial record in the tempo and character that suits the director. What you use does not make any difference as long as it is replaced in the final product. This track or record is used only to establish tempo for the dancers. The record can be kept running for the extras to dance to, until dialogue. Just before dialogue starts, the track must be cut off and the dancers keep dancing as close to the established tempo as they can. If the track were to continue, it would be recorded along with the dialogue. Any picture cuts that would be made in a dialogue scene with music running would "jump" the music. It is always necessary to keep the dialogue clean of anything that would restrict the final editing. The start of the guide track should be recorded with whatever dialogue set up is working. Although you will replace this "leakage" track, hearing it up to dialogue makes it easier for you to break down. It is much easier to establish tempo from such a "leak track" than it is from just watching the movements of the dancers on a Moviola.

What is better still, is the use of a "tempo track". The tempo track is a record of a click loop in the desired tempo. The playback operator plays this click record at the start of each part of the scene. The tempo track not only gives you a dead set tempo for the dancers to work to, but it sets up your post scoring tempo then and there. Most commercial records tend to drift, as far as tempo goes. A tempo track is absolutely accurate and insures your not having any variation of tempo in your post scoring routine. Most directors do not like tempo tracks. They feel that they have no character, which is true. If the establishment of tempo is very short before the dialogue starts, try to sell the idea of the tempo track. It will save you some time later on. All of this should be carefully explained to the director before shooting. During the shooting, he should have the right to decide as to what serves the picture best. One word of caution about tempo tracks: even though you may use them to shoot with, you will still have to check the final cut carefully to make sure that the tempo didn't change during filming, or that the editor didn't cut the picture out of synch. If he did, find the place where it occurred and have him add or subtract the few frames that are necessary to bring the picture and the dancers back into synch.

CHAPTER 2

PRODUCTION PROCEDURES

#1—LIP SYNCH OF THE ARTIST

When the time comes to shoot the sequence that you have pre-recorded, a music cutter — or you — should be on the stage to check lip synch. Whomever takes charge of lip synch should be positioned alongside the camera with a good view of the artist. Make sure that the artist is actually singing along with the pre-recorded track. Just mouthing the words doesn't look right as it does not involve the throat muscles that are used in singing. Make sure that the playback level is high enough to give the artist something to lean on. The main idea in covering lip synch is to be sure that you get a visual picture that looks right with the pre-recorded track. If you have the vocal on a separate track, you can settle for a somewhat rubbery performance. The vocal track, if separate, can be moved a bit to conform to picture. The process of frame cutting is really better handled by an experienced music cutter, but the premise of this book has been to assume that you are completely without help. If you decide to frame cut a vocal yourself, be sure and work with a print off of the master take! Never work with the original track. If you ruin a track, it is an easy matter to get another printed off of the original. When cutting a vocal, as described in the previous chapter, work with the orchestra track and the vocal track lined up in the synch machine. Mark the frames on each track before you do any cutting so you have progressive points of reference to return to as you cut. Always check the cut track from the top against the music track to be sure that you have stayed in relative synch.

If you are working to a monaural track, you will have to get the best overall take possible. If time allows, get at least two. Take into consideration that in the finished picture you can cut back and forth between two or more takes with ease. Also, the director may have reaction shots or off stage stray shots going during the number. These are cutaways from the vocal and can be placed where the vocal synch might be especially bad. Often times, you will have to settle for a performance that is less than great. The press of time may force the director to continue on, even though the vocal take wasn't necessarily good. It is at these times that the value of a separate vocal track becomes important. A good music cutter can unobtrusively chop out the center of words to sharpen synch. Production procedures will always take precedence over yours. Get the best track, visually, that you can and do the best you can to make it work.

#2—STANDARD RECORDING ON THE STAGE

It is justifiable sometimes to record "Standard." This means that the recording and photographing are done simultaneously. Three-camera television shows like "I Love Lucy", and "The Danny Thomas Show" were always recorded standard. The set was usually a night club and the usage of microphones on the stage were logical. This enables you to get some kind of balance. It never is as good as a true recording studio, but it eliminates the necessity for pre-recording and/or post recording of numbers. The only problem is that you are stuck with what is shot. If there is a vocal goof or orchestra mistake involved in the shooting, you have to cut picture to make a cut in the track.

On a three-camera show, this can be done because there are always two more camera angles to cut to. If you are working with an organized group that is well rehearsed and has its set repertoire, then it may well be alright to recommend the usage of standard recording. Try to get a fairly decent recording set-up on the stage. If microphones are allowable in the scene, by all means use as many as your mixing panel on the stage will allow. There usually aren't more than three or four mike inputs on a stage mixing console that is designed for dialogue recording. Try to place what mikes you have to your best possible advantage. If the scene doesn't allow for visual mikes, try to get the director to shoot his overall master in the closest possible set up so as to allow you to get your mikes in close. It is almost a must to have a "Playback-recorder" on the stage whenever you record standard. This machine can not only be used for playing back, but it can be used for recording the master as well. The Playback-recorder is an acetate cutting machine that is synch pulse operated. It will cut a record of the master as you shoot it. This record can be played back for all of the pickups that the director wants to make. The musicians can play along with the record or sideline it (appear to be playing). A synch pulse tape recorder can also be used both ways.

Occasionally, in the pure interest of saving money by eliminating a pre-recording session, you may have to plan to record something standard. Hire the best musicians available and write parts out for them. It doesn't pay to have musicians faking while the camera is rolling. If it is a fake type of group that is involved, at least give them a roadmap kind of arrangement that is right for length and time and is organized to cover the scene. You have to keep in mind that you are going to be stuck with anything that you recorded standard so get as good sounding a track as you can.

#3—SIDELINE MUSICIANS

If any track is to be photographed in front of or involving the appearance of live musicians, you will have to hire a sideline combination. Some conversation will have to take place with the director as to the type and appearance of the musicians he wishes to photograph. These musicians do not actually play; they merely go through the physical movements of the pre-recorded track or guide track without making a sound. They are there to be photographed, not recorded. If they were to play audibly while being "shot", they would have to stop playing and continue the motions while the dialogue is being recorded. The rate of pay for side line musicians is much less than for recording musicians. Always discuss the scenes involved with the director. You might actually record with forty year old musicians, but if he wants to show teenagers, cast for type. A call to your local musician's union will usually help you to get the personnel you need. If you are using a music contractor, you can turn this job over to him.

#4—PROCEDURES FOR USING GUIDE TRACKS, TEMPO TRACKS, PRE-RECORDED TRACKS

The playback procedure in all cases is the same. Make sure that the necessary discs are on the filming stage the morning that they work. Get a copy of the shooting schedule, or find out from the assistant director what the sequence of scenes will be and line up your discs to work that way. You can help the playback operator mark his starts and from that time on, you are in a supervisory capacity. The playback operator, by union law, is the only one allowed to handle the playback machine. Make sure that the recordist picks up a few bars of "leak track" (the start of the number) to make the job of post-synching easier. If for some reason the guide track doesn't satisfy the "on stage" needs, the sideline orchestra can play something to start the dancers. As long as you don't use their recorded track in the final picture, it becomes a "temp track" and you only have to pay for sideline. If for some reason you do decide to use their track in the final picture, you must pay them the difference between sideline pay and recording pay. Again, a call to the union will help you figure the overage. Just make sure that _no_ music gets recorded under dialogue. A common case would be that of a bugler playing a call. You may want to use it or not. Until you decide to use it, it remains a temp track. These situations of actually using recorded music that was not planned for do not happen often. Keep them in the "if" realm and make your decision when the times comes to post-score.

CHAPTER 3

POST-PRODUCTION PROCEDURES

#1—ASSEMBLY OF PRE-RECORDED TRACKS

All pre-recorded tracks should be synchronized to picture and placed in the reel according to matching footage. The picture you will be working with will usually be a "dupe" (a cheap print off of the dailies that is assembled into a working print). The negative itself is never touched until all phases of the work are finished. Then the negative is cut to match the work print or dupe and sent to the laboratory for final optical print. All picture cuts should be checked against the original pre-recorded music tracks to make sure that they were edited in synch. If the film has been opened up anywhere in a number to lengthen a scene, the space to be filled out should be leadered out and measured to be "padded" in post-scoring.

#2—THE COMPLETE BREAKDOWN

Generally a running with the producer and/or the director should be scheduled for an exchange of ideas. You should run the picture at least once before you meet to discuss the problems with the producer or the director. It is always a good idea to have at least an outline of the approach to the music job before getting into deep discussion. After you have run with the producer or director, or both, you should set up a reel-by-reel running with your music cutter. It is at this running that you formulate your stops and starts and set the general policy for the musical approach to the picture. This does not mean that you can't change your mind as you work. It also does not mean that the producer has finalized his picture.

Cutting and trimming may continue as you work and you may find yourself having to make timing changes and cue changes right up to the recording date. It can be frustrating to have a cue well conceived and get hit with a last minute change that forces you to work hard at repairing the structure of the music affected. This is one of the less happy circumstances that you run into. If the producer feels that the change is vital to the picture you might as well accept it and work to make it come out right musically. I have never heard of a producer or director that did not win this particular battle, so make the best of it. The best way to work, if you have the time, is to sketch the scenes that might be affected and not orchestrate them until the last possible moment before recording. In some extreme cases the changes may take place after the picture is completely finished. If this happens you will have to do remakes on the scenes involved or cut the music tracks to fit.

After breaking down the picture the cutter starts making your cue sheets and bar breakdowns. The interim between breaking down and getting your first timings can be used to start working out thematic material. By now you have seen the picture a few times and should have a pretty good idea of your musical burden. Upon the completion of the entire breakdown for cue sheets and bar breakdowns the cutter should prepare a bible for you. This bible is a complete list of all of the cues in the picture on a reel by reel basis. This is your check sheet. If you cross off the cues as you complete them, you will have a running account of the cues that you have completed and the cues you have yet to finish. Your copyist should have a copy of the bible and check the cues off as he completes the copying. This allows you to keep track of all of the elements going on as you approach the recording date. Because the recording stage and musicians have to be booked in advance, the bible is an absolute must.

The average time allowed for the composition of a feature is six weeks from the date the film is turned over to you for your first running. One hour T.V. is usually two weeks, 1/2 hour T.V. one week. These are only averages. Film scores have been turned out in every amount of time from two weeks to one year. T.V. composers are often faced with a deadline of a few days. If you figure the time lost in preparation of cue sheets, timings, etc. you can also see how time itself has a habit of shrinking on you. As you complete your cues, the information necessary to set the film up for recording should be given to the cutter for stage preparation. All technical information should be passed on by you or your copyist so that the set-up of clicks and punches and streamers can be in preparation as you continue to write the score. If you decide to split a cue, be sure to pass the information on to the cutter and enter it on the bible. A split cue usually has the second half of the cue designated as "A" (M11 and M11A; M26/31 and M26/31A). The appearance of an "A" cue may involve a complete change of recording set up. Give the cutter all of the pertinent information. If a cue is split into more than one part, you designate the split as "A"-"B"-"C"-etc. Without every bit of information as to what you are doing the cutter cannot properly prepare the film for recording. If you decide to use a click instead of free timing, give the cutter the details of the cue and state how many warning clicks you wish. It is easier by far to have the recording date well prepared than to run into snags on the recording stage.

Keep close check on the bible as to your work output. The recording date is a commitment. It must be met. If you are stalled on a cue, pass it. You can always come back to it at a later time. By then you may have developed some original material that will open the cue up for you to sail through. There is no set procedure for composition. Some composers like to start from the top and develop the music in sequence. Others like to skip around, often starting with the hardest cues first, or the key cues that expose material that can be used throughout the score. This operation is extremely personal and it really makes no difference how you do it as long as it works for you.

#3—THE RECORDING

You should put out the call for musicians at the earliest opportunity. The best players are booked far in advance and if you wait until the last minute to call your players, you may be sadly disappointed. If you do not know which musicians are best, the investment in hiring a good musical contractor can pay large dividends in terms of performance and time saved. It is the business of the musical contractor to know who the fine players are. The best players save you time and money, give your music the best chance to be heard properly and cost no more than the poorest. Having the best players is the finest investment you can make toward the end result.

Some time before the actual recording date you should contact the recording engineer, give him the orchestra set-up, and put in a request for whatever equipment you will need. You are the only one who knows what musical problems are developing and what you may need to expedite them. If you have a contractor, he can assume the burden of securing whatever you need in recording equipment—but, you must tell him. It really is better if you take care of these problems yourself. That way you will know that everything will be covered. All it takes is a phone call.

As far as the actual recording goes, you should start with the largest recording set-up you have. There is no necessity to record in picture sequence. By recording your largest groups first you can continue to cut your orchestra down as your orchestrations get smaller. This means that as you approach the period of overtime, where music gets expensive, you will be working with smaller groups. Besides costing less, it reduces the burden on the engineer and allows him to function more efficiently. Again, these are considerations of cost factors, but the musical director's responsibilities include cost along with everything else. Sound planning helps hold budgets down and should yield greater returns in quality. Time that is poorly spent is reflected in loss of quality and a rise in expense. If you have prepared well, there should be a minimum loss of time, money, and most importantly, quality.

Most picture composers like to start their date with the main title. The main title, or opening credits of a picture, is similar in psychology to the keynote speech at a political convention. It sets the tone and tenor of things to come and is generally an important piece of music for the film. It is a good policy to proceed with the picture cues first. Picture cues are generally a heavier burden for conducting as they involve music that is flexible in content; they consume more time on the stage and it is good common sense practice to get them out of the way while the orchestra is fresh. After you have completed the picture cues, you should go to the click tracks and then, last of all, to the wild cues. If you have no further cues that involve picture or clicks with smaller combinations, you can dismiss the projectionist and dummy operators when you start your wild cues.

If you have trick set-ups for recording, put them all together so that once you have achieved a good recording approach you can go through all of the cues involving the same technique without having to change your recording set-up. These are short cuts to save time and trouble—all of them have been tried—all of them work. Any kind of preparation that can save you time and trouble is worthwhile. It will make itself felt in greater quality with less panic.

If you are working to stopwatch only, have the cutter check the critical timings as you record. If you miss some of these, you might be able to make a "pick up" instead of having to do the whole cue over again from the top. The same thing applies to clicks. Once you have checked your first take to picture and assured yourself that the cues are right, you can go to the digital click machine or a matching click loop and record the whole cue, or any part of it, without having to use projection or click track. A click track that is especially built for a sequence will run out at the end of the sequence. If you have a mistake, either in playing or recording, you have to wait until the track is rewound and put back into a dummy machine before you can make another take. If you are sure that the cue fits, go to the usage of a loop. It never ends. You can make partial or complete takes of a cue by simply counting of a warning bar or two. These pickups are very easy to "intercut" because of the steady tempo of the click loop. If you are operating totally without projection, make one good overall take and whatever pickups that are necessary.

Most recording stages have the digital metronome. There are two methods that the cutter uses to start the digital machine. One method is where the cutter gives himself a red streamer to start the machine for the warning clicks. This method is not necessarily accurate. If the cutter pushes the start button slightly early or late, the whole cue will be slightly off. If you see, for example, that all of the cues seem to be slightly late or early, you can ask for the playback to be slowed or advanced a few frames. That usually will pull the cue back into synch. The second method is to have the projectionist notch the film for an automatic start. Studios that have that facility usually charge $50 a reel.

Have your copyist set up the orchestra books with the largest orchestra first and then a constantly reducing orchestra pattern throughout the whole date. This sequence should be given to the cutter, who, in turn, makes copies of it and gives them to the recordist, the engineer, the projectionist and the dummy operator. In this way, everyone knows what cue is coming up and can be prepared for it.

Hold on to any men who are involved in "Sweeteners". By union law, they must be recorded at the end of the date. When you finish with your sweetener tracks, you will be through with the recording date.

EXAMPLE #47 The Author at Work On Stage "M"
Glen Glenn Sound Co.
Paramount Studios — Hollywood, Calif.

EXAMPLE #48

From the Orchestra Point of View

#4—PREPARING FOR DUBBING

After the recording, you should work with the music cutter while he makes any intercuts in the tracks. Make sure that all intercuts are smooth and fit the picture. From your bible and your take numbers you can make a cue sheet log to turn over to music legal. If the producing company has a legal department, they will prepare the cue sheet forms and rights assignments. If you retain the publishing rights, make sure that all copyrights are registered and that the producing company has however many copies of the registered copyrights as they feel necessary.

When all of the music tracks are cut together and built into music reels, you are prepared for "Dubbing". Music that overlaps from one cue to another will be built on two separate reels. The cue that starts will be on a reel designated as an "A" reel. The cue that takes over at the overlap will be leadered out to the point of overlap and then laid into take over at that point. This cue is on a reel designated "B". The two reels are placed in separate dummies and run simultaneously. If there are a lot of musical starts and stops in a reel, they will be staggered between the "A" and "B" reels. It is possible that sweeteners and overlays might be built on "C" and/or "D" reels. The cutter can use as many reels as it necessary to keep the music going simultaneously. Unlike the record industry, in film recording the tracks are never cut together except for intercuts within a cue. Music tracks are mounted on "A" and "B" reels and overlaps are crossed over from one reel to another rather than cut together. This gives the film composer some extra frames to work with on his musical crossovers. It also allows the dubbing mixer to preadjust his levels and notate them on his dubbing cue sheet. In physically recording the music it might be necessary to have a completely different recording level from one section of a piece of music that overlaps to another. By having them on two reels the levels can be set so that the end re-recording level is exactly the same and the overlap becomes unnoticeable.

#5—DUBBING (RE-RECORDING)

In the glossary of this book, Dubbing is defined as: "The re-recording of all aural tracks—dialogue, sound effects and music, for the purpose of arriving at one track incorporating the mixture of all aural elements to be optically printed on the finished film". It is that, and more. Dubbing is the next to last step in picture making. The last step is to cut the negative, make the prints, and ship them.

To understand the mechanics as well as the complicated psychology of dubbing, it should be broken down into two completely different types of functions.

234

**EXAMPLE #49   Re-recording and Dubbing Stage E.
Glen Glenn Sound, Paramount Studios, Hollywood, Calif.**

EXAMPLE #50   The Re-recording Console

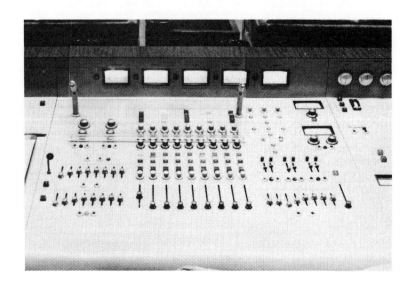

EXAMPLE #51   The Dialogue Mixing Panel

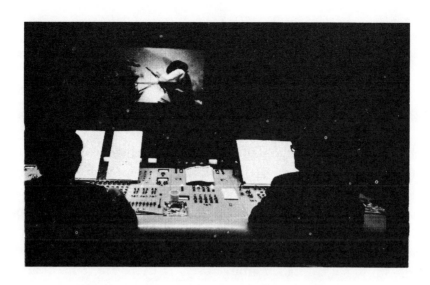

EXAMPLE #52   Dubbing Mixer At Work

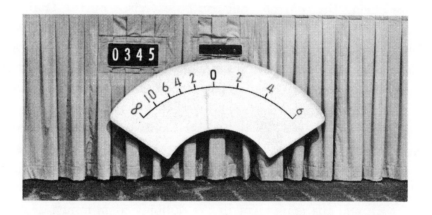

EXAMPLE #53   Footage Counter and Overall Level DB Meter

EXAMPLE #54   Dubbing Machine Room

A.—THE MECHANICS OF DUBBING

Example #50 shows a dubbing console in one of the fine independent sound services companies, Glen Glenn Sound Co. of Hollywood. As you can see, this console has three identical banks of re-recording panels. A sound mixer operates the right bank, the dialogue mixer, who is usually in charge of the mechanical procedures, operates the center bank, and a music mixer operates the left bank.

Most T.V. dubbing is handled with two men. The dialogue mixer also handles the music tracks. Each mixer can handle up to six tracks simultaneously. If there are more than six tracks, or if there are more units running than can be handled by the available manpower, the surplus tracks can be divided among the other mixers. If a sequence is too involved with multiple tracks to be handled, it can be pre-combined. This means that any two or more tracks can be re-recorded into one track before the actual dubbing to picture starts. This pre-combining procedure is usually done with picture so as to get the proper perspective. Equalization, attenuation, suppression, compression, and limiting of recorded tracks are among the controls that can be exercised on the final product. Each mixer is usually handling two or more tracks. Sound effects may have two built reels of sound effects running, and a couple of effects loops going at the same time. These effects loops are loops of specified sounds: birds, subway backgrounds, restaurant background effects, etc. These loops may run all through a take and be dialed in where needed. The dialogue tracks are generally lined up on "A" and "B" reels so that lines that have been recorded in different perspectives can be equalized and balanced to produce an even effect. The music mixer will be working with two basic reels and perhaps a third reel containing sweeteners, overlays, or special effects cues that require reverberation or special handling. Normal room tone reverberation is generally added at the time of recording but for special musical effects, the best place to experiment is the dubbing room. You do not have the expense of the orchestra to contend with and the equipment in the dubbing room is just as complete. Doing special effects this way also allows you to balance the musical effect with the rest of the picture components.

Adjacent to the dubbing room is a projection room and a machine room containing enough dummy machines to cover the needs of the three mixers. These operate the same way as for recording except in dubbing, the material is fed to the dubbing console.

Each mixer has prepared for him a dubbing card. This card contains all of the information as to the cues in the reel and the footage at which they occur. All starts and stops are indicated on this dubbing card. A large footage counter is located in front of the screen and can be seen easily by the three dubbing mixers.

The reel to be dubbed is rehearsed until all of the components are in proper balance, then the crew starts to make takes. This particular console has a "Back-up Recorder" which allows the dubbing crew to stop anywhere, back up twenty feet or so, and then start forward. Once the machines are up to speed, the dialogue mixer can throw a recording switch and you are recording the take again with no noticeable crossover. A half hour T.V. show is usually dubbed in three hours or less, an hour show in six hours or less, and a feature film in a week to four weeks depending on the length of the film and its inherent problems. Six track stereo movies can take as long as several months to dub. Musical extravaganzas are also among the longer dubbing sessions.

The dubbing room is the room where all the mechanical imperfections are cured. Noisy splices, overlaps in dialogue, or inequities in recording of any type are cured in dubbing. Tracks that are out of synch are re-aligned. This is the last place that any repairs can be made. It is common to have to cut and repair tracks in dubbing. The film editor, sound effects cutter, and music cutter are usually present in dubbing and available to make the necessary corrections.

This is the basic mechanical concept of dubbing. All of the procedures that go into the making of a picture are funneled into this room to be put together into the final product.

B.—*THE PSYCHOLOGY OF DUBBING*

Psychologically speaking, the dubbing stage is a chamber of horrors and a total frustration to the composer. This is the room where you will hear your music over, and over, and over again until you hate every note of it. It is in this room where marvelous effect that you conceived and recorded gets wiped out by a tire squeal. This is the room where you will encounter the laugh track for the first time. It is here where you will eventually get up and scream, "What happened to the music?"

Most of the time, your complaints will be met with blank stares. Sooner or later you will hear one of the mixers say as you walk in, "Here comes that guy again, all he cares about is the music". You will find yourself arguing about the values that your music can give the picture if they just give you enough level to be heard. Most of the time you will be unsuccessful. Eventually you will begin to collect some information about dubbing. You will realize some hard facts about theatrical musical life.

First of all, there can only be one hundred per-cent put on a sound track. You cannot say that you want ten percent more music level without getting someone else—sound effects or dialogue—to give up ten percent. Secondly, all dubbing mixers protect dialogue. This is their bread and butter, and rightly so. All of the aesthetic values are in the hands of the producer, who has the final say, or an associate of the producer who has invested in him the authority to make decisions. If there is a key-note in dubbing, it is compromise. You will, sooner or later, learn to compromise in your orchestration and try to overcome the losses that you know you are going to suffer in dubbing. Pertinent facts, like the existence of a mysterious ogre called "The Academy Roll-Off" will begin to seep into your technique. Optical film, to which the final product is transferred, has a much more limited range of recording than the original mag tracks. In order to keep the optical print from distorting, all frequencies above 7500 cycles are cut off. As the dubbing level is dropped under dialogue, the juicy bass notes you have labored over begin to dissipate, and the academy roll-off takes the live "presence" out of your music. This is fact and has to be accepted. You will find yourself starting to load the bass end of the orchestra to strengthen it, and it will work. Your orchestration will become leaner or stronger behind scenes where there are known sound effects or principal dialogue. The unison will be more effective behind a situation that you know will be covered by a laugh track. You will find that, in dubbing your product, a couple of steps of low equalization will bring back the loss of the bass register, and a boost in E.Q. at 5000 cycles will restore some of the presence that you will lose because of the academy roll-off. Little by little, if you can make it through a few dubbing sessions without considering suicide, you will begin to accumulate the information of what works, and what doesn't. In the final analysis, it is the end effect that the music makes that decides whether you have been successful or not. If you can learn what you have to know about the end product at which you must arrive, you are on your way to becoming a picture composer. This can all be accomplished without sacrificing the integrity or aesthetic qualities you wish to express in your music. The film industry has limitations. These limitations are placed upon you, the composer, as they are on every other facet of art and craft. As you learn the limitations of the medium, the word "practical" will take on a less dirty meaning, and you will find that you can achieve fine results without giving up anything in which you believe.

Dubbing can be a rough exeprience and a disappointing one, but don't think for one minute that it is a dead loss. It isn't. Many wonderful scores have been written for the film industry and been completely handleable.

Attending dubbing sessions is a must and will help you gain control over your medium. The total concept of what has to take place in the picture beside music is something that every good film composer must develop. If you have an idea that will supplant a sound effect or an extraneous line of dialogue, try to sell the idea to whomever is going to be in charge of dubbing, before you write it. Try to express your idea not in terms of music, per se, but in terms of the theatrical value your idea can achieve for the scene. The time to do this is before you record, and before the sound effects editor or dialogue cutter has spent a great deal of time building an effect that you want to replace. If you can learn to describe your intentions in terms of theatrics, your chances of succeeding by the time you get into dubbing will be greater.

Don't forget, music is an intangible. It is not a door slam, or a gun shot, or a spoken word. Most of the time it will be impossible for you to explain the values you wish your music to express in a given scene. A producer or director, to fully understand you, would have to have a musical background. This is not common. Say it in terms of theatre. This he will understand. The time to say it musically is on the stage when you record. The place to make it stick is in dubbing.

The techniques of film making are changing. Brought on by experimental films in Europe and stimulated by the foreign film, producers search to find other ways to state their picture premises other than the literal. Imagination is starting to be accepted as a standard picture form of expression. Cutting styles are becoming vivid in their execution. The usage of sound effects in an artistic manner (rather than the literal approach of "See a street car, hear a street car") is becoming more sought after and totally accepted. Music is being given the chance to flower, as long as it has something to say.

Long gone are the old days of showing a radio on the screen so everyone would know where the scoring was coming from. You can be as daring in your work as your imagination, and the film, allows. Whatever you do, don't waste your time trying to convince a dubbing mixer of the aesthetic values of your approach. Like you, he operates in the field of service. The difference is that his service function is primarily in the area of mechanics and yours is in the field of aesthetics. Your primary obligation is to the people who have hired you. These are the people to whom you must direct your creative flow. If you know your picture—if you know the values inherent in the film—if you have kept yourself aware of the problems of dialogue and sound—chances are that you can outguess the frailities, lean on the strong points, and express yourself musically in terms of good picture making.

Dubbing need not be a nightmare. It need not be dull. A great deal of what kind of experience it will be depends on the man who is in charge. If he is firm in his opinions and knows what he is trying to get as an end result, he will more than likely get a good product. If he is unsure of himself, he will be exposed to a myriad of opinions on every facet of the film from everyone in the dubbing room. This has to lead to confusion. Plenty of picture values have been lost in the dubbing room because the man in charge was not flexible enough to listen to and appraise helpful suggestions, or not strong enough to disregard those that were invalid. By the same token, many pictures have been helped enormously by astute mixers with plenty of experience, and creative people working in a creative manner.

Example #55   The Dubbing Room In Operation.

(Note The Projection Booth Above The Mixing Console)

CHAPTER 4

LISTENING TO THE END RESULT

The preview, in the motion picture business, and listening at home to the television show you have written, have the same function. They give you the opportunity to hear the end result in the environment for which they were intended. Pictures with small budgets do not generally have previews. The sole purpose of the preview is to try out the film with a live audience and, by their reactions (both in the theater and on cards they are given to fill out), determine the success of the film, or find the places that are weak and possibly repairable. This too, can be a harrowing experience. The beautiful silky low end of the orchestra is suddenly absorbed by the carpets, seats, and the clothing of the people in the theater. The environment has unexplainably gone dead, and everything sounds dull. For days, or weeks, you have been listening to the product in a hard floored, acoustically perfect, dubbing room. The level of everything has been high and hot. The level in the dubbing room is always kept high to catch poor splices in any of the recorded material, and to give the dubbing mixers the chance to find any extraneous noise on any of the tracks. The atmosphere in the dubbing room during takes is dead silent. In the theater, all that seems to come through is the rustling of popcorn bags and the coughing of the audience. The drop in level from dubbing to theater is enough to throw you off balance; and the extreme absorption of the environment tends to make everything sound as though it were filtered through cotton. Most of this feeling is psychological—some of it is not. The best you can do for yourself is to listen. Listen objectively and critically. Listen and learn. Make written or mental notes about every device you have used that works, or does not work. Later on, when you get a chance to re-evaluate the preview, you can determine whether anything that semed weak was due to dubbing procedure, or just poor writing. The chances are that after preview there will be some re-dubbing, or re-takes and re-cutting. If there are re-takes, you might have to rewrite some of the music and go back for another recording session. The amended product will then go back into dubbing. At that time, you can make any suggestions that will help strengthen areas that you felt were weak in the original preview. It is not unusual for a picture to have several previews and a good deal of reworking before it is shipped for final release. If your picture is not previewed, go to see it in the theater on a crowded night. Take stock of the effectiveness of your contribution and be critical of the areas that you feel could have been better. It won't help you on this particular picture, but can be of great benefit to you for the future.

If you are working in T.V., you won't have the opportunity to make repairs. Most T.V. shows have an answer print running as soon as the negative is cut and the picture has gone through the lab. It is a good idea to attend these runnings if you can. Sometimes there are dubbing repairs to be made and you can redo a section that turns out wrong. Most of the time the film will be shipped immediately. There just isn't enough time in T.V. for drastic remakes. The best experience is to watch the film at home. You will find, once again, that the environment is quite different than the dubbing room. The ambient background noise of the home is very strong. Trucks going by, the refrigerator motor, the washing machine, the kids hollering, and the dog barking — all of these common sounds compete with, and tend to destroy, the music you have written. Beside the noise in the house, you have to contend with the station monitor. Each transmitting studio has an engineer who watches a meter to be sure that the volume being transmitted does not exceed F.C.C. limits. He will often anticipate a climax and turn the overall level down at a crucial moment. About the time you get the level on your set back up to where it sounds normal, the commercial comes on and slams you against the far wall. Or so it seems. Once again, some of this is psychological and some of it is not. The final product in T.V. suffers much more than in the theater. By the time your product has been recorded, re-recorded, subjected to the academy roll-off, transferred to optical, printed, duplicated, transmitted and received in the home on a four inch speaker, you will swear that there is no music left on the track. Unquestionably, the final music product has suffered — but only in relationship to the overall product. It is easier to detect the loss in music than in dialogue because dialogue has a limited range in the spectrum of sound, and the small speaker in your home set is particularly effective in the dialogue range. The medium of TV is composed of a certain amount of loss. Listen to your product objectively. Analyze the end product carefully and try to strengthen any noticeable weakness in your writing. Then make a point of going to the next dubbing session armed with a little more knowledge about how to achieve an end result that is effective in the home, which is the only place where your musical contribution to T.V. counts.

* * *

SUMMARY

To the best of my knowledge, this text has covered all of the mechanical and psychological problems to which you, the composer, will be exposed.

Composing for film has many rewards. Not all of them take place in the theater or on the air. The greatest reward takes place on the recording stage when for the first time an orchestra breathes life into the music you have created. It is on the recording stage where you achieve the fulfillment of the need to express yourself. Don't kid yourself for a minute that you are writing music to satisfy anyone but yourself. If, in so doing, you can satisfy the people who hire you, your future in this business is secure.

This security comes from within, because it reflects not what you have earned or saved, but rather what you can do.

ACKNOWLEDGEMENT

I should like to express my gratitude to one of the most outstanding music cutters in our profession, Mr. Ken Johnson. I have had the good fortune to have a long and happy association with Mr. Johnson and his help as Devil's Advocate in the mechanical sections of this book were invaluable to me. He has also been a stalwart source of reference to the pupils I have taught and to the best of my knowledge has never turned one of them down when they have approached him for "on the spot" help. His cutting room door has always been open to them for some "over the shoulder" experience.

I should also like to pay my respects to my long time friend and colleague, Mr. Hugo Friedhofer, who is one of the true giants in the motion picture field. I am indeed privileged to have his permisison to use some of the examples of his music in this book.

I must also acknowledge the help I received from an associate of long standing, Mr. Carl Brandt, one of the most capable and gifted composers in our business. His technical and musical contribution was of inestimable value to me and I am deeply indebted to him.

All photographs courtesy of Glen Glenn Sound Company, Hollywood, Calif.

GLOSSARY OF FILM TERMINOLOGY

#1   *ABBREVIATIONS*

F.I.   *Fade In*

The picture starts from a full frame of black and, over a period of 3 feet or more, lightens into the full frame of picture. It is possible that movement or action may be taking place as the picture fades in.

F.O.   *Fade Out*

The reverse process of going from picture to black.

F.F.O.   *Full Fade Out*

The end of the act, or the end of the picture.

F.O.-F.I.   *Fade Out-Fade In*

An optical effect used in place of a dissolve to indicate a change of time or place. It most generally is used to denote lapse of time, especially when the location does not change.

DISS.   *Dissolve*

The photographic process of bleeding one scene into another. In T.V. this is generally done in a period of three feet. The movie industry uses six feet as a norm, but dissolves of up to fifty feet, for lingering effects, are not uncommon.

CUT.   *Cut*

The editing process of splicing one shot to another, forming an instantaneous change of location, point of view, or angle.

C.U.   *Close Up*
Camera location.

B.C.U.   *Big Close Up*
Camera location.

PAN. *Panning Shot*
The movement of the camera horizontally or vertically to expose scenery or cover location.

O.S. *Off Stage*
This usually refers to dialogue.

M.S. *Medium Shot*
Camera location.

F.S. *Full Shot*
Camera location.

L.S. *Long Shot*
Camera location.

M.L.S. *Medium Long Shot*
Camera location.

C.S. *Close Shot*
Camera location.

F.O. TO COMM. *Fade Out to Commercial 1/2 Second Allowed*
The Fade Out to the end of an act or the end of the picture. The 1/2 second allowed gives the natural reverberation of the last chord time to die away. If this allowance were not made, the music would sound chopped off as the negative is cut off on the final frame of black.

E.C.U. *Extreme Close Up*
Camera location.

CUT TO INT. *Cut To Interior*
Change of location.

CUT TO EXT. *Cut To Exterior*
Change of location.

M.T.	*Main Title*

The signature music that accompanies the opening credits. In the present day technique of using some story before the credits, this is not necessarily the first piece of music in the picture.

E.T.	*End Title*

The final music cue in a picture.

These are the most common abbreviations. Others may be devised by your music cutter or by yourself. If you do not understand any abbreviation on a cue sheet, by all means get a clarification.

#2   *BAR BREAKDOWN*

The picture information set on music paper to a click track and indicating all vital information as it happens. See Example #10.

#3   *BIBLE*

The Master List of the entire show. See Example #12.

#4   *"BUILDING"*

The physical process of assembling all tracks for dubbing. This process is handled by the music cutter.

#5   *CLEAN*

The process of recording dialogue where any music track is cut off to avoid being picked up.

#6   *CLICK TRACKS*

A film metronome that can be locked in synch with the picture.

Written Click Tracks

The method of writing bars of music in even values in lieu of having or wanting click track facilities. See Example #19.

Variable Click Tracks

Any click track where the basic time unit either speeds up or slows down.

Special Click Tracks

A click track where the normal unit has been divided in unusual ways to allow more creative expression. See Example #15.

#7   *COMBINE*

The process of reducing two or more tracks down to one. This process usually takes place before dubbing. For examples—Chapter #3 —Page 236.

#8   *DEAD CUE*

A self-imposed picture obligation that you have decided to accent with music.

#9   *DOUBLE TRACKING*

A music sequence designed to contain two or more complete music tracks running simultaneously.

#10   *DUBBING*

The re-recording of all aural tracks—dialogue, sound effects and music for the purpose of arriving at one track incorporating the mixture of all aural elements to be optically printed on the finished film.

#11   *DUMMIES*

35 MM playback machines that lock into synch with the projector. See Example #4

#12   *DROP-OUTS*

Imperfections in the oxide coating of the recording tape or film that cause distortion or momentary loss of level.

#13   *GUIDE TRACKS*

Any track that can be used by the producing company to service its on-stage needs. Guide tracks are always replaced.

#14   *INSERT*

A film device for close point of view. If a man looks at his watch and then you have a shot of the dial of the watch showing the exact time, that shot would more than likely be an insert. The importance of this is that inserts are usually shot after the regular shooting schedule. This means that in breaking down your film, you will often run into blank leader marked "Insert." This leader has to be taken into account for timing purposes and there will be any number of times when the dramatic highlight falls on an insert.

#15   *INTERCUT*

The process of editing music for removal of mistakes, corrections in timings or improvement of performance. The music cutter must mark the tracks to be cut and check them to be sure that they remain in synch.

#16   *LOOPS*

A click track that has been spliced together at the ends. When placed in a Moviola or dummy machine, it runs continuously, providing a steady, never-ending beat. Those loops can be punched for optical use, or scribed for magnetic use.

#17   *MAG.*

The abbreviation for magnetic film of any kind. Full coat, single stripe and ¼″ are all used for the recording of music, sound effects and dialogue.

#18   *OPTICAL TRACK*

A track that is motivated by a light valve and a photo-electric cell rather than a mag head. See Example #1.

#19   *OVERLAP*

The process of tying two music cues together. See Chapter 12.

#20   *OVERLAYS*

Musical effects recorded over a basic music track.

#21   *PLAYBACK*

A record of a previously recorded vocal, dance or instrumental routine. This record is used on the filming stage when shooting the sequence.

#22   *POTS*

The level controls on the recording console.

#23   *PRE-RECORDING*

Any track that is recorded before filming.

#24   *PUNCHES*

Bursts of light that have been punched into film for the purpose of keeping the conductor oriented to the music.

#25   *PICK-UPS*

Short sections of recording that can be intercut to eliminate mistakes in performance, timing or recording.

#26 SAFETY VALVES

The name given to any musical device that allows the conductor some leeway to pick up his dead cues.

#27 SIDELINE

Visual orchestras who give the appearance of playing, but do not. See Chapter 2—Book 3—Page 225.

#28 SPLIT CHANNEL RECORDING

The method of recording vocal and orchestra simultaneously but with each entity going to a separate recording machine. It can also be achieved on a single stereo machine by sending the vocal to one of three stripes. The main feature of split channel recording is that the vocal track can be edited without touching the orchestra track. If any editing is to be done to a three stripe vocal, the vocal stripe should be first transferred to a single stripe track.

#29 SPOTTING

The process of deciding where music is to start and stop.

#30 SNEAK START

A start of any music cue that is brought in under a sound effect. If no sound effect is available, the orchestra should make the most unobtrusive entrance possible.

#31 START MARK

A notation on the film, usually white tape, that is placed 20 feet ahead of the actual beginning of the cue allowing all the machines to reach proper recording speed.

#32 STREAMER

A line scribed on the film that visually guides the composer to a dead cue.

#33 SWEETENER

Any added musical effect that can be recorded separately to ease the recording burden.

#34 SYNCH PULSE

An electrical device to lock non-synch driven motors into synch with the camera or projectors. A 60 cycle tone is laid down the center of the mag recording tape. Any change in line voltage would affect the 60 cycle tone exactly the same as the camera or projector.

#35 *TIMINGS*

> This usually refers to the cue sheet which contains all pertinent information regarding the sequence and the split second timings that take place.

#36 *TAPPING*

> The method of tapping the film in the movieola with a white grease pencil to provide a basic visual click track for sequences that are uneven.

#37 *TRACKING*

> Scoring a picture from a pre-recorded library of music.

#38 *WARNING CLICKS*

> In normal or slow music, two bars of clicks preceding the first bar of music and in the amount of the tempo of the first bar. If the first bar of music is in 4/4, you would have eight warning clicks. If the music is very fast, you would be better off having four bars of warning clicks-i.e., 16 clicks warning.

#39 *WILD*

> Any music recorded to stop watch only. It is possible, and common, to record a whole picture wild.

#40 *WORK PRINT*

> A cheap duplicate of the cut version of the picture that can be marked, scribed and used for cueing purposes.

#41 *ZOOM*

> A camera effect that comes in from a fixed position or moves back from a fixed position. This effect is usually accomplished by a fixed focus variable telescopic lens.

EARLE HAGEN

ABOUT THE AUTHOR

EARLE HAGEN started his professional writing career when he was stationed in The Santa Ana Air Force Orchestra for over three years. After a year of freelancing in the record business as an arranger and conductor, he went to work in 1946 as an arranger/orchestrator for Alfred Newman at Twentieth Century-Fox Studios. In 1953, Mr. Hagen turned to the budding field of television where (with the exception of two feature films) he has remained until retiring in 1986. Mr. Hagen has scored more than 3,000 television episodes. He won an Emmy for Original Composition in 1967 for his score to "Laya," an episode of I SPY.

In 1971, he wrote SCORING FOR FILMS, the book that has become the standard film-scoring text for universities and colleges all over the country. His latest book, ADVANCED SCORING FOR FILM, emphasizes multiple reel recording. Recently, he established the Earl Hagen Workshop for Film Scoring for B.M.I.

In retirement, Mr. Hagen still teaches the B.M.I. workshop twice a year. He and his wife, Lou, live in Palm Springs, California, where he enjoys the good weather and a plethora of golf courses.

The last two television shows Mr. Hagen wrote music for were RETURN TO MAYBERRY and THE RETURN OF MICKEY SPILLANE'S MIKE HAMMER. RETURN TO MAYBERRY was the third most-watched show in the history of television. MIKE HAMMER featured a theme, "Harlem Nocturne," which was composed by Mr. Hagen at the age of 19.

COMPACT DISC PROGRAM
Music Segments from the Actual Film Sound Tracks
(conducted and narrated by Earle Hagen)
Ⓟ Ⓒ 1971 E. D. J. Music, Inc.

1 Introduction (:35)

2 **Ex. 13A, 14A** (2:24)

3 Combine of **Ex. 13A & 14A** (2:17)

4 **Ex. 15A**—The listesso click track (1:28)

5 **Ex. 17A**—Free timing to stopwatch (1:13)

6 **Ex. 19**—The effect of orchestration on tempo (1:17)

7 **Ex. 21**—Picture cueing (1:31)

8 **Ex. 23A**—Picture cueing conducted to stopwatch (1:46)

9 **Ex. 24A**—Freedom of tempo changes in picture cueing (2:21)

10 **Ex. 25A**—Combination cue, clicks to free timing (1:40)

11 **Ex. 28A** pt. 1, pt. 2 (1:45)

12 Combine of **Ex. 28A** pt. 1 & pt. 2—The overlap from click track to click track (:50)

13 **Ex. 29A** pt. 1, pt. 2 (2:12)

14 Combine of **Ex. 29A** pt. 1 & pt. 2—The overlap from free timing to free timing (1:07)

15 **Ex. 31** pt. 1, pt. 2 (2:15)

16 Combine of **Ex. 31** pt. 1 & pt. 2—The overlap from clicks to free timing (1:53)

17 **Ex. 32**—Effects overlay track recorded echo return only (1:41)

18 **Ex. 33**—Basic track and 10 overlays (1:54)

19 Combine of **Ex. 33**—Overlays cut into basic track (:40)

20 **Ex. 34** track 1, track 2 (3:03)

21 Combine of **Ex. 34** track 1 & track 2—Double tracking (1:03)

22 **Ex. 34A**—Double tracking (3:29)

23 **Ex. 36**—Scoring under dialogue with the use of clicks (2:06)

24 **Ex. 39**—Free scoring in and out of dialogue (1:27)

Note: [A][A][D] Analogue tape recorder used during session recording and subsequent mixing and/or editing; digital tape recorder used during mastering (transcription). Original analogue source contains imperfections which may become apparent on this digital disc.